WHY DID WE JOIN?

First published in 2003 by
WOODFIELD PUBLISHING
Bognor Regis, West Sussex, England
www.woodfieldpublishing.com

ISBN 1-903953-53-7

Why Did We Join?

A Former Waaf Remembers
Service Life in World War II

EILEEN SMITH

Woodfield

WAAF Eileen Smith, April 1944 intake, Wilmslow Training Camp
(the cap had not yet had 'the treatment'!).

CONTENTS

~ ~

I dedicate this book to my family who have had to
put up with my WAAF stories over the years.

~ ~

1941 – My friend Betty (right) and I,
wearing our Women's Junior Air Corps uniforms.

1. We Are At War

We children had had an idyllic summer holiday from school, bike riding, swimming, playing on the giant strides and swings in the local park and looking forward to going back to school to meet up with our friends.

We knew our parents had been watching the newspapers and listening to the wireless and finally September 3rd brought the dreaded news from the Prime Minister that we were at war with Germany.

We realised from the looks on older people's faces that a dreadful thing was happening and everything we had known was going to change.

My school friend Eileen and I had been awarded a scholarship to Hendon Technical Institute (later College). We were fourteen and looking forward to tennis on the courts, hockey on the field (and scoring the winning the goals for our schools) – all things we had read in our *Girls Own* annuals – but of course it didn't happen like that.

All projects not related to the 'war effort' were abandoned and we had letters from the Education Department telling us that we would not be attending the college as it was not completed. They suggested we look for work.

Eileen and I were stunned; work hadn't come into our plans, although in those days 14 was the accepted age to begin work if one was not going on to further education.

I didn't want to go out to work, I wanted to learn to be a secretary, but Mum decided to do the rounds locally and see if something could be found for me.

I had an interview at a local drapery store for a shop assistant. I opened the door of the drapery to a loud clang from the metal bell above. It was a gloomy shop, stocked to the ceiling with materials: skeins of wool, cotton reels, thimbles, needles, cards of combs, ribbons, mending wools and in the glass case below, gloves, handkerchiefs and scarves. Behind the counter stood a tall, thin lady in drab clothes, she wore tiny, round, steel-rimmed spectacles, her fair hair was dragged back in a scalp-pulling style to the back of her neck, where it was fastened with a huge clip.

As Mum and I waited, she carried on serving a customer, took the person's money, undid a screwed-on object attached to an overhead wire and sent it along the wire to a window, where another person took out the bill and money then sent it back the same way, with a receipt and change. Today it sounds slow and cumbersome but I wonder if, for all the high-tech equipment at point of sale, it is any quicker by the time the card has been put into the machine, key-in the pin number, wait for acceptance, print out a long bill etc…

I was now ready for my interview. I wasn't enthusiastic and I think it must have shown, because the lady wasn't at all keen on having me work with her and so we left the dingy little shop and outside in the bright sunshine I heaved a sigh of relief – I was free… That was, until Mum took me to Bon Marché on the High Street.

The window dresser had arranged the *directoire* knickers in a provocative way, the whalebone corsets were set at a jaunty angle, the stockings in their see-through envelopes displayed invitingly and the vests sat comfortably on the wide-eyed "model".

Once more I sat on a hard chair answering questions and Madam said she would "let us know". I was pleased to learn that the vacancy had been filled.

I pleaded with my parents to wait a while to see if the college re-opened and they agreed, so I had reprieve for several weeks.

In the meantime Dad had put up the Anderson shelter in the garden. Finchley was very much an area for clay and it was a hard job to dig the shelter into the solid ground, but eventually it was done and covered with soil – on which a flowering creeper would soon grow.

Preparations for war were now in progress. Millions of children were evacuated to safer areas, some to live in the country. As many of them had never travelled further than their own towns they were at first quite at a loss as to how to cope with the quiet of the countryside. But the country people were wonderful and opened up their homes to both children and adults.

We were all issued with gas masks and I can still recall that dreadful smell as one pulled the rubber mask over one's head. They were placed in a cardboard box and a string was tied to the box. We were never to leave home without them and so we were constantly reminded, "Have you got your hanky and your gas mask" and in the evening "…and your torch".

The blackout was in force and not a chink of light was to be shown. Mum managed to get hold of some black material and we sewed a few rows of coloured tape at the base just to brighten them up. Bicycle lamps were hardly visible and cars had their lights dimmed, that is, what few cars there were, as petrol was rationed.

At last came a letter from the Education Department that the college was going to re-open and so uniforms were purchased from Gamages. We sported the three daggers of Middlesex with wings above, as our college overlooked Hendon Aerodrome. This badge was lovingly stitched on our blazers and hat bands.

The course was for two years and during that time we learnt office procedures, shorthand and typing, bookkeeping and all the usual subjects. Some boys learnt woodwork, metalwork, etc in another building.

This was a two-storey building and when an air raid was in progress a bugle would sound and we would make our way down to the corridors and sit on the floor, under the windows till the all clear, finishing the lesson there.

We had disruptions all through the two years and on one occasion had incendiary bombs dropped on the classrooms, burning holes in the new desks.

At times we could go home early if we had had only a couple of hours sleep and we would sometimes do our homework on the bus and in the shelters. But in spite of Hitler, we did get an education!

Before the war, our family had never had a holiday in the country or by the sea. Dad was the breadwinner, there were seven of us in the family, myself, four brothers and Mum and Dad. Expensive holidays were out of the question. We did have a wonderful day by the sea with the Sunday school outing. This was usually by coach or train; Southend-on-Sea or Clacton were the main venues.

We would return home red-faced from the sun, sandy and happy, carrying our buckets of water and shells, looking forward to yet another wonderful day next year.

Part of defence was to barb wire the beaches and install huge concrete blocks to prevent enemy tanks landing. Most people stayed at home for their holidays but some of us took advantage of a scheme called "Give A Hand On The Land".

2. Giving A Hand On The Land

Men and women of all walks of life could contribute to the war effort by helping to produce food. The workers would pay a very nominal amount for board out of the farm wages which were paid for the work and at the same time enjoy a breath of fresh country air, away from the bombing and disturbed sleep.

I went with Mum, leaving Dad behind to look after my three younger brothers. My eldest brother, Den, was now in the RAF. I was sixteen when we had this break. I enjoyed the hard, back-breaking work out in the fields, sitting on boxes with a roll of string tied to my belt, pinching out the sweet, pungent-smelling lateral growths from tomato plants, the minty smell clinging to my hands. I enjoyed the companionship of the other men and women, who came from all parts of the country.

Most of us came prepared for the sort of work we would be doing, but others, especially the city girls, arrived in high-heeled shoes, stockings and fine clothes. If they had no other suitable garments, others would help them out with items from their own suitcases.

We slept in huge canvas tents, ate in communal tents and washed in cold water from white enamel bowls. I had taken some Pears Transparent soap for my own personal use and for ever after, the smell of that particular soap brought back memories of sitting out there in the field, far from the bombing, enjoying a joke with new friends.

There were six to a tent. In ours there was myself, Mother and four young women, business girls who came to "Give A Hand On The Land". There was much laughter in our tent and in the evenings, the girls would make for the village and would meet up with some Canadian soldiers who were on manoeuvres in the area, their tanks hidden among the nearby woods. They would enjoy their evening and crawl back late, lifting the sides of the tent and giggling, feel around for their beds. The 'beds' were straw-filled sacks laid straight onto the ground. We were all 'townies' and in the morning we were staggered to find hills of soil in the tent, mole hills. They had been burrowing their way inside the tent while we slept.

In the mornings we were awakened by a loud "Wakey, Wakey, Rise and Shine!" and a big stick was whacked on the side of our tents. We made haste to dress in our old working clothes (if we had brought them with us) and hurried to the mess tent to be served with a hot breakfast and hot strong tea in the biggest mug we could bring.

We then waited by the gate for farmers in the scheme to pick up as many workers as they needed for the crop and then transport us by lorry to their farm.

It was great, sitting up in the lorry, being driven along country lanes, singing, laughing and looking forward to the day. It happened to be a good time of the year and the sun shone most of the time. One very wet day we were taken to a potato crop and with sacks over our heads we sloshed through the mud, following the harvester, picking up the new potatoes and filling the sacks and boxes. It was hard work, but lunchtime made up for it. Lunch consisted of sandwiches, mostly cheese, in great thick slices. I think there must have been special rations for farm workers like ourselves as we hadn't seen this much cheese in years. My mother even used the rind when grating cheese. The bread was cut in big "door-steps" and the tea, out of an urn brought down from the farmhouse, was strong and thick and lots of it.

Sitting there under the hawthorn hedgerow in the midday sun it was as near to heaven as it could be. We hadn't a care in the world, the war was far away.

Our camp was in a beautiful part of the country and a river meandered along nearby. In the evenings, after the days work, a wash and into clean clothes, we would walk along the grassy banks, watching dragonflies swooping low over the glass-like surface of the water, weaving and ducking to catch their evening meal.

There were ducks with their young, gliding majestically across the water and boys sitting by the water's edge on the bank with their home-made fishing rods, using the very same method I had used when my brothers and I would take a lunch with us to a local farm and fish for sticklebacks. We would find a long piece of twig, a length of cotton or wool tied to it with a matchstick a few inches from the end as a float and on the end a small piece of wriggling worm as bait, hoping to catch another stickleback to join the others in the jam jar.

At our camp I made friends with Sam, a quiet boy of about 17, he was dark haired and had soft dark eyes. He asked me if I would like to have a boat out for a row one evening. He had come to Give A Hand On The Land with his father and, like us, was enjoying the time away from the routine of college and sleepless nights.

I sat in the rowing boat, the sun was setting and casting wonderful lights on the rippling waters and I hoped it was also turning my shoulder length wavy brown hair into spun gold.

"Give me your jacket Sam," I said, "I'll look after it," and reaching out without causing too much movement in the little boat I reached out for it... but in doing so the contents of his pocket slid out and disappeared over the side and into the depths of the Thames! I was mortified, how stupid I felt, but he was so nice about it and said, "You know Eileen, you remind me of a very fascinating cow we once had. She had soft brown eyes like yours."

I didn't know what to say to this compliment, probably the best I had ever had, and smiled, thanking him for being nice over his belongings. After the row we had a lemonade at the local pub, joining others from our camp in the pub gardens.

By the time we returned to our homes in the city we felt rejuvenated and were much more knowledgeable about farming and country life.

I had completed the two years course at Hendon and was now ready to earn my living. We had all grown into our uniforms, filling out the blouse top which had rows of gathers for growing girls and with meagre coupon rations we fitted ourselves out for our jobs. I wore the same outfit for over a year (washed of course at the appropriate time!). I recall it was a plaid skirt in red, white and fawn check, a white, pristine blouse and a red mohair jacket.

When we had completed our course it was the practice of the Education Department to ask local businesses to visit the colleges and let the young people know what sort of jobs were available and in fact offer some to people if they were at all interested.

The headmaster, who got to know me when I was chosen to be his private secretary for the week, suggested I may like to work in a bank as I was "a quiet girl". I may have been quiet and very shy but no, working in a bank did not appeal to me!

Finally I gained a position as junior secretary to a manager of several newsagents. I liked the work, the office was above a busy newsagents and I spent my days taking dictation, typing and counting endless rows of figures without the aid of a calculator – good job we had counting "tots" at school. With my small wage I was able to buy a few more clothes and enjoyed buying make-up and all the things a 17-year-old wants.

The next job offered to me was at the company where my grandfather worked – a tyre re-treading and re-capping company. The position was for a junior short-hand typist for the Company Accountant, Mr Finnegan, a tall Scot who was great to work with and from whom I learnt a lot.

The company sold new and re-treaded tyres and with the war well in progress had a Government Contract. I was in charge of the paperwork and it was so confusing. Each order involved about six pieces of paper, colour-coded, but the problem was that the yellow page was marked "blue copy" and the red page "pink copy" – don't ask me why, it was a mystery, but then it was a Government department that organized it!

My office was lovely; it had been a boardroom and the timber-lined walls had prints of the "old masters". We would have our lunch at the desk and lunch was one of the best things about the job. Mrs Brown, a rosy-checked and plump lady was the cook. Every day for the time I was working there she made super hot lunches and puddings, always a scrumptious raspberry jam tart with custard and the coffee was also superb. As the youngest office worker, I was asked to take the trays of food into the managers' offices. I didn't mind; it was a break from the office.

It was 1942 and women were now being 'called up'. Gradually, most of the females in my office went and although invoice typing was done by two middle-aged ladies who had been hired to help out, I had to take on the work of all the others who had left. I was drowning under a sea of paper. Apart from letters, I had to make the books balance for the different sizes of tyre from small to TT (Tractor Type) and had to account for the in and out movements of all the tyres. But, nothing would balance. I was gradually losing the plot.

My saviour was Mr Haas, a lovely white-haired German Jew, who had been roughly taken from his bed in Germany, made to stand with his wife in the snow in pyjamas for hours then bundled into a truck and on to a concentration camp. I don't know how it was done but the owner of the company I worked for, also Jewish, managed to get Mr and Mrs Haas out of Germany and gave him work. Mr Haas spoke good English and it was he who worked through the mountain of paper with me and finally discovered that the tyres had been "falling off the back of the lorry", which was why, of course, the books wouldn't balance!

However, after seeing one of our Hendon girls in her natty Naval uniform singing "There'll Always be an England" at our college concert our hearts swelled with pride and I decided that I too would join the WRNS.

Giving a hand on the land – Laleham Park 1943.

A friend from Sheffield who I met at the camp.

3. Wilmslow

My mother agreed to take me to the Naval Recruiting Officer but when interviewed they offered me the chance of becoming a cook. No, no, this wasn't what I wanted at all! I declined and we made an appointment with the WAAF Recruiting Officer instead. In due course I was sitting in front of the officer, filling forms, answering questions, putting little round blocks of wood in little round holes and performing other "tests" to try and find out what use I could be to the WAAF.

Looking back now with the advantage of maturity, I realise that I should have taken the opportunity to learn something new. I should have joined the Motor Transport Unit, I could have learnt to drive, after all, one couldn't get lost in a convoy, but no, I said I wanted to stay where I could use my skills and so it was decided I would be a Clerk SD (Special Duties).

Later we were to have our medical examination and I passed A1, feeling sorry for the girls who were not accepted, either with something like flat feet or for more serious disabilities.

I received my calling up date just before my 19th birthday. A fairly new blanket, a lovely shade of apple green was cut up to make me a cosy dressing gown, all the usual things like comb, brush, make-up, writing paper and pen were packed and I made my way to Kingsway in London.

Sitting in the crowded room of the Recruiting Centre my thoughts were "What will it be like? Will I like it? Why am I here?" Gazing around the room, we were a motley crew, most of us in our late teens and early twenties. It was early 1944 and we were late arrivals in the war, which had begun in September 1939. Now was our chance to 'do our bit' and to see some action.

We clutched our luggage with all our belongings and anything which could be marked was either printed or embroidered with my new WAAF number – 2170298 – the last three numbers being the important ones.

As I looked round the room I noticed a small, plumpish girl with bright brown eyes and rosy red cheeks, her hair short and curling wildly over her head. Next to her was a tall, gaunt girl with huge eyes staring out of her almost skeleton-like face, the cheekbones all but pushing out of her taut skin.

'I've got to talk to someone, got to make a friend, it would all seem much better if I could share these moments with someone,' I said to myself. I walked over to the brown-eyed girl and said, "Wonder how long it's going to take before we're on our way. My name's Eileen."

"I'm Squibs, that's my nickname, everybody calls me that and this is Barbara." She put her hand out and touched the sleeve of the tall girl I had been looking at. Barbara looked relieved.

"Fair old game this, ain't it?" she said in her strong Cockney accent. "Wonder what it'll be like there, I mean, at Wilmslow."

We all looked relieved, we had broken the ice, made contact, we were a little nucleus. As we chatted I heard the Sergeant bellowing and realized she was directing her shouting at me above the noise. Me? Why me? Why was she addressing me?

I could feel all eyes on me, accusing eyes. 'Who does she think she is?' they seemed silently to be saying.

The Sergeant continued "You there!"

"Me?" I said.

"Yes, you, you look a sensible girl, I'm putting you in charge of this intake – look after the paperwork and see that everyone here gets to Manchester where you will be met by someone from Wilmslow."

I felt my face turning red, my hands were shaking and my heart beating so loudly in my ears that I could hardly hear. I just couldn't believe she had picked me out me to do the job.

First lesson, do as you are told without question.

"Right, you're on your way now Smith, remember what I said, all get there in one piece."

We all climbed on to the waiting lorry and were driven to the Railway Station. I held the papers in a vice-like grip and glanced nervously at the others girls scrambling for their seats on the train. I had enquired from the porter if this was the train for Manchester and was told, "Change at Crewe".

My charges, once the train slowly moved out the station, rushed along the corridor, whistling and calling to the passing men, giving the distinct impression that it had been years since they had seen a man, where in fact it had been just a few hours since they left home.

We all settled down in the crowded train, the carriages packed and the corridors filled with people, mostly service personnel, sitting, standing and smoking, their kitbags making it an almost impossible to wend one's way to the toilet.

At Crewe, the station smelling of fish from boxes filled with the day's catch, piled on the platform waiting to be dispatched to all corners of the country, the voice of a female announcer shrilly announced, "The train standing on platform two is due to leave in five minutes and will be stopping at all stations to Manchester".

There was a banging of train doors, people saying desperate goodbyes, waving of hands, crying and then, slowly, the train edged its way along the platform, meandered through the jungle of interwoven lines and out into the open country and onwards towards Manchester.

By some miracle we all managed to change trains without loss of one member. We were on our way. Soon we would be in Wilmslow and well-and-truly part of the WAAF.

"Next station Manchester!" called the ticket collector as he made his stumbling way, stepping over service personnel who hadn't managed to get a seat and were sitting in the corridor on their kit bags and cases.

I stood up and took the paperwork out of my handbag as I had a travel warrant to cover our group.

Stepping out of the carriage and making an effort to get our London intake together we heard a voice barking "Come on you Sprogs, get a move on, can't wait all day!"

A stiff-backed sergeant was striding along outside the ticket collector's gate. I handed him the paperwork with a sigh of relief and he marshalled us into a waiting truck. We made our way through the dingy streets of Manchester, looking like any other big city, but through the green and lush countryside toward Wilmslow it was like another world, untouched, it seemed, by the war.

As we approached Wilmslow WAAF Training Centre, we could see Waafs being drilled, some marching some square bashing. We must all have felt just a little stir of fear of the unknown approaching. What would it be like? No parents to guide us, no one to give us help with any personal decisions, just us and our officers and NCOs.

We were marched, or I should say pushed, in the direction of a huge hanger, where we were told to wait until we were given our hut numbers. We were probably one of the last intakes to arrive here as it was 1944 and unbeknown to us, the war was to finish in Europe the following year. We were sitting around in little groups waiting to hear our names called and the number of our allotted huts. "Smith 298, Hut 18," and so on. We were all together, Squibs, Barbara and myself. We were shunted into some sort of order and taken to hut 18.

Hut 18 was long, bare and held beds down both sides. On the wire base were three square mattresses or "biscuits" which, when placed on the bed, made one hard mattress. There were blankets, sheets and a pillowcase for the hard, sausage-like pillow. Corporal gave us brief instructions as to how the bed was to be made and how to stack it in the morning for hut inspection. After that we were told, "Meal in about 20 minutes girls".

We unpacked our belongings, placing them in the allotted drawers of a shared chest and then turned to the business of bed-making.

During my years in the WAAF I rarely finished up in the morning with all three biscuits together and my bottom had the distinct markings from the wire base, looking not unlike a waffle.

When we were all assembled in front of the hut, our Corporal, a short, sturdy lady of around 30 years of age with thick red wavy hair, ordered us into some kind of formation and marched us off to the cookhouse, en route stopping at the Equipment Store for our issue of 'irons' – knife, fork and spoon – and a sturdy mug.

The Mess Hall was large and contained long trestle tables and bench-type seating. We joined other Waafs shuffling slowly round the walls toward the serving counters. As we moved along, we read the graffiti on the walls: 'Betty Brown, London 1942', 'Jean Martin, Leicester 1943' and so on. The walls were thick with messages from girls who had passed this way before us.

I reached the first cook, who stood behind the long counter, menacing a ladle.

"Hold yer plate out… Spuds?"

"Yes please," I quietly replied and - splot! Down came a dollop of soft mashed potatoes.

"Sausages?"

"Yes please" I said and at high speed two brown sausages came hurtling in the direction of my plate.

"Gravy luv?" said a smiling, short, plump Waaf cook with her hair pushed under her white cap. I nodded.

Splosh! Dinner was complete, with the brown gooey gravy fondly caressing my sausage and mash.

Next was the tricky bit.

"Pudding?"

"Yes please"

"OK, put yer puddin' out for treacle."

Puzzled, I looked hard at the cook and she grinned. Later I was to learn this line had been used since the beginning of time and so, with one hand holding my dinner plate and the other holding the pudding plate which held tinned fruit and custard I dangled my mug from my finger and made for the centre of the Mess where there was a large tea urn.

If one was unlucky enough to receive the last dregs of tea, by tipping up the urn for the last drop, a gooey sludge would slowly ooze from the tap, we were told, and "Oh yes, they put Bromide in the tea to keep those nasty romantic feelings surging forward".

I am pleased to say, that on this first occasion there was no need to tilt up the urn and so, with the two plates in one hand and a mug of tea in the other, I slowly made my way to the trestle table where Babs and Squibs had saved a place for me.

We had to sit close together to fit onto the bench and those who were in the habit of eating with their elbows out at an angle found it necessary to bring them tightly down at their sides.

Arriving at my seat I made several attempts to cock my leg over the bench without splitting my skirt from stem to stern. Once seated, I took the pudding plate from beneath the dinner plate only to find the pudding had stuck on the top plate. Ugh!

Dinner over, we went to our hut, spent some time sorting things out and settled down to talking and learning a little more about each other. It had been a long day, we had left a comfortable home and now shared our bedroom with 19 or more women.

Hardly, it seemed, had our heads touched the bullet of a pillow than we were rudely awakened with the Tannoy blasting out reveille - it seemed to say "get out of bed get out of bed you lazy ...." I sat up and saw through bleary eyes all the activity.

There were always the "go getters" they had to be first no matter what. They rushed to the ablutions for their wash. I crawled out of bed and followed, I'm not and never have been, an early riser and in fact have always declared that only milkmaids and servants get up early. I did my ablutions, brushed my hair, which was still shoulder length as we were still wearing 'civvies', although I knew I would have to do something with it to get if off my collar when I had a uniform or I'd be 'on a charge'.

I returned to my bed space and proceeded with difficulty to keep any form of modesty by going into all sorts of contortions. There was one girl in our hut, a very top-drawer girl, and she undressed right down to the altogether and we, after our initial shock gave claps and cat calls. From then on she too learnt to dress in such a fashion as to not bare her all.

Now it was bed-making practice. I stripped the bed, placed the three biscuit mattresses on top of one another at the head of the bed, folded a blanket lengthwise into four and, placing this on the bed, folded the other blanket and sheets into squares, placing them alternately, one sheet, one blanket, one sheet. The long folded blanket was wrapped around these squares, making one gigantic liquorice allsort.

Time for breakfast, and once more we filed toward the row of cooks behind the counter. It was egg and fried bread today. There were huge doorsteps of bread and big lumps of margarine. I put my plate out and on the piece of bread was placed a rubber-like white egg with a hard yellow centre. It didn't look good but it tasted great, and at our age we couldn't get enough to eat.

After breakfast Corporal made an inspection of our beds, making suggestions here and there as to how we could improve on the finished result. We were to be at Wilmslow for a month doing lectures, drilling and finally a Passing Out Parade. Here we were to get our grounding ready for our individual postings to other RAF stations.

Today was Kitting Up day. We entered a huge gaping opening in a hangar and saw rows of tables and each one was manned by either a WAAF or RAF person.

First we were each given a long sausage-shaped kit bag, a gas cape and a ground sheet, gas respirator and a steel helmet. Then as we moved along the counter we collected:

- 1 cap badge – in brass
- 2 jackets 1 for work and one for best (Best blue)
- 2 skirts – straight and shapeless.
- shirts – without collars.
- collars
- 1 tie

- 1 long sleeved cardigan
- 1 pair woollen gloves
- 2 pair of shoes (as the song goes "Dammed great boots make blisters on your feet. Why did we join ....)
- pair thick grey lisle stockings
- 1 pair blue slacks (leisure and PT)
- 2 pair knickers
- 1 dark blue ("blackouts") or passion killers as they were called
- 1 pale blue silk like pair ("twilights")
- 2 vests
- 2 suspender belts
- 2 brassiers - in thick pink cotton – absolutely shapeless. If we had any notion of producing the shapely pointed bosom a la Lana Turner we were sadly mistaken. These issue would only produce two flat bulky blobs under a manly shirt.
- 2 towels
- 1 housewife pronounced hussif, for sewing and mending
- 1 pkt. Sanitary towels. We were told Lord Nuffield, as a gesture to help women in the armed services paid for the supply of these towels. We were very thankful for this, they also came in very handy not only for the job they were meant for but for polishing floors, covering the eyes when trying to sleep – the loops reaching the ears and at Christmas, the contents, little bits of cotton could be placed along the rough rafters above to give a festive look of snow flakes.
- 1 button stick

- 2 identity disks made out of salmon pink coloured bakelite with name and number inscribed in case of the necessity of identity for death or injury.
- 1 hairbrush.

By now we were staggering under the weight of full kit. We collected our hat and two pair of shoes then made our way back to the huts.

I was average build and at that time average height 5ft 6½ ins but we all differed in statistics and so some of the uniforms had to be altered. Some of the intake could be seen in mixed civvy clothes and uniform while waiting for the altered garment to come back.

Meanwhile we soon made the uniform smart. We pressed four pleats into the straight skirt and the very small WAAF made us laugh when they put the "one size fits all" knickers on and pulled the waist up to under the armpits and the legs down to their ankles. I think these could almost be called *directoire* knickers!

The following hours were spent in marking our new issue with either pen or embroidering with needle and thread. It was a tedious job marking everything with our service number but a good way of impressing it on our minds forever. Finally, when the job was completed the kit was laid out on the bed for inspection.

Of course it all looked and smelled new. The hat was a big give away that we were "sprogs". The crown stood up like a bakers hat and the peak was straight and guards-man-like.

We soon learnt a few "old soldiers" tricks such as wetting the hat and pressing it flat to make it look much more used. The peak would be bent, with difficulty, slightly over the face and set at a more jaunty angle.

We now felt we were IN.

Next was the cap badge. Being new it had sharp defined edges and with a nail file these edges were honed down to a smooth appearance and worked on till they shone.

When our issue became frayed over the years and the stockings were mended until little of the original material was visible, we could return them to Equipment for replacement. It was a very acceptable way of obtaining new clothes and shoes etc. and eventually on returning to civvy street we found it difficult to part with our money for new stockings, etc.

The following day we were to receive our inoculations for Tetanus and some other nasty sounding diseases. We queued in the Medical section, sleeves rolled up above the elbow waiting for the jab. The girl in front of me flinched as the long needle entered her arm and then it was my turn. I was told to place my hand on my hip and I turned my head away as I felt the sting of the needle and my eyes smart.

Later back in the hut sitting on our beds feeling sorry for ourselves, our corporal asked each one of us how we felt and dished out aspirins if she felt we needed one. It was several days before the dull ache disappeared.

The next day we were assembled in a large hanger and we were addressed by the WAAF CO. She told us what was expected of us, how to behave, how to dress and then proceeded to tell us that there were American soldiers in the village nearby, saying "Now gals, I want no necking down the lane, we want no fraternizing".

She went on about general conduct in and out of barracks, told us of the Secrecy Act and that what we were going to see and hear during our Service time we were not to impart to anyone not even our family. Of course we had seen the posters on walls, trains and buses "Careless talk costs Lives", "Do What Dad Does – Keep Mum" and so on and therefore we were aware of the real necessity of keeping our mouths tight shut.

Now that we were kitted out and most of us had full uniform we were due to start drill. I had been fortunate in already knowing most of the drill movements as my friend Betty and I, at aged 16, had volunteered for the Women's Junior Air Corps. Our uniform consisted of a straight grey skirt, blue/grey shirt, a tie, grey stockings, black shoes and top it all off a natty grey forage cap.

An army NCO from a nearby Territorial Army unit took us for drill in a large playground of a local school and we soon became proficient at marching, countermarching and saluting. We learnt aircraft spotting, we learnt to distinguish different types of gases should they be used by the enemy, we also learnt Morse Code.

I did hear of a friend of mine who had such poor eyesight so she told me, that she was desperate to join the services and learnt the eye test letters by heart. She told me she passed and went into the Army. It was not detected that she had poor eyesight and therefore she kept quiet when her first posting was to an ack-ack post and the mind boggles as to any result there may have been with her at the helm. Her next posting was to assist with aircraft spotting. Methinks her story should be taken with a grain of salt!

Morse code was taught us by an ex-Post Office lady. Half a dozen of us went to her house and we sat round a table in her front room, a chenille cover probably protecting a lovely timber surface. We all had an ancient Morse Tapper. We were taught the code, how to tap out .- ..- ... and so on. She told us that everyone had their own signature, that a trained ear could know who was sending a message.

The Junior Air Corps was putting a band together and I dearly wanted to play the drum, but even in those days it was not what you know but who you know and as I told Mum, "You should have invited the WJA chief to tea and then I may have got into the band".

We had all the corporals, sergeants etc and my friend Betty, a small plump girl and myself appeared to be the only privates. We marched, swung our arms and the NCO shouted to Betty to "lift those arms". I was 5ft 6in and Betty was 5ft 1in and to keep in line with my arm she had to lift hers higher and higher. These drills were to come in handy for me as, later, when entering the WAAF I was to miss out on much of the "square bashing".

So at last we were going to be made into a smart WAAF and so assembled on the parade ground. The young eager RAF corporal looked at us with glee. Here was a rough bunch! He'd soon get us into some form of order...

"Right girls, form a line, shortest on the left, tallest on the right and then form three lines... Come on! Haven't got all day!" And so we shuffled, changed places and then it was … "By the left … quick march, left right, left right, left right, swing those arms, thumbs close to your index finger, higher, heads up, shoulders back, etc" and so it went on. Gradually we leant to march in an orderly fashion: right wheeling, left wheeling, saluting eyes left and right, open order marching until finally it was 'Der Tag' – the day when we were good enough to air ourselves to the public.

We had been in camp for just one week and were looking forward to the march. We were going on a route march through the streets of Wilmslow town and out into the adjoining countryside. "Tallest on the right, shortest on the left," screamed the corporal.

'Drat!' I thought, 'I'm one of the tallest. I'll be in the front row.' Later, when markers were called for on the parade ground I would bend my knees a little under my skirt and shrink, thereby missing the "honour" of being chosen. We formed into three rows and, by stretching out our right arms to touch the shoulder of our neighbour, shuffled into straight lines. The order "right turn, forward march" was given and we were off down the path, through the gate and to freedom. "Left right, left right, keep in step…" I loved marching, it was not a chore for me; I enjoyed hearing our footsteps unison.

We hummed quietly to ourselves as we marched through the country lanes:

> *"Why did we join, why did we join,*
> *Why did we join the Royal Air Force?*
> *Ten bob a week, nothing to eat,*
> *Damn great boots, make blisters on yer feet…"*

"Left right, left right, swing those arms!" bellowed the corporal as we swung our way along the roads, into the village where shoppers hardly gave us a passing glance. They were used to seeing marchers, they had more pressing things on their minds such as how much meat, if any, they could buy today with their ration books and were there any rabbits off the ration to be had.

It is just as well we had this route march as the following week we were confined to barracks as most of the basin plugs had been stolen. No one would own up to the dastardly act and so everyone was confined to barracks. For the remainder of my WAAF days I carried a penny tied in a handkerchief, which just fitted into most basins and I was even able to use this "plug" when staying with friends or at guest houses where plugs had mysteriously disappeared. There was a shortage of rubber, it being used for the war effort, so such things as plugs were considered not necessary.

We must have been marching for hours but I'm sure we improved step by step and mile after mile.

We returned to Wilmslow tired and hungry and after a wash and tidy up made our way to the NAAFI for a cup of tea and possibly a custard tart.

Lectures continued through the weeks until one day, listening and taking notes, the lecture ceased when an orderly approached the Officer on the dais. She gave a message quietly, looking important and then the Officer said, "Oh dear, very well". Looking up from her notes with an annoyed frown she said, "298 Smith, you are wanted at the Medical Office. Quickly girl, hurry".

My heart thumped against my ribs as I gathered my notebook and handbag, the whole assembly by now eyeing me with interest. I brushed past the sitting girls and followed the orderly to the Medical Officer's office.

"Sit down Smith," said the doctor.

I must have looked worried and upset. He tried to help by saying, "Just a little problem with your X-ray. You may have moved and we need to do another."

'Thank goodness,' I thought, 'it wasn't serious' and so I undressed, pressed my shoulder to the cold plate, held my breath and waited to be told I could take a breath again.

The MO did not think I would be needed again. I was told to rejoin the lecture.

I was called again to the MO next day and as I sat in front of him he shuffled his papers and then looked at me saying, "There's something not quite right on your X-ray. We don't fully understand what it is. I want you to be admitted to camp hospital for a few tests."

I felt quite sick. What could be the trouble? My thoughts were racing, I would have to miss drill, lectures, the Passing Out parade, all this went through my mind as I made my way back to the hut to collect my Small Kit, that is, pyjamas, change of underwear and shirts. I was told to place all my other kit into a holding bay.

I put my shoes, underwear, jacket, greatcoat etc into the sausage-like kitbag, putting my name clearly on a tag and took it to the Nissen hut where I was told it would stay until I was released from hospital.

Wilmslow Training Camp 1944 intake. Author 4th from left, middle row. 'Squibs' first on left, top row. 'Babs' last on middle row.

'Squibs (above) and 'Babs', who both joined in London, April 1944 intake.

4. In Dock

The hospital was sparkling clean, a smell of carbolic pervading the air. I was put into a large ward, told to have a shower and get into bed.

I was in a daze, it had all happened so quickly. I had passed my medical A1+, felt fit and looked healthy and rosy cheeked. Climbing into the high ward bed I looked about me. Other Waafs had also be recalled by the MO as their X-rays had not been good and were in the hospital for tests. Tuberculosis was suspected. I spoke to the girl in the next bed who had been told she had a slight mark on the X-ray and that she had tuberculosis. She was being discharged from the WAAF.

I was anxious to know what my problem was and certainly prayed that I would not be discharged too. Not only would I lose the chance of serving in the WAAF but also there was the awful thought, apart from the illness, of going back home after making my goodbyes.

I found out that the Polish Air Force girls had been in a ship which had been torpedoed in the North Sea and they had been in the sea long enough to give them pleurisy and other chest and lung ailments.

I went for more x-rays and other tests and meanwhile began to enjoy the comforts of a slightly softer mattress, softer sheets and nicer food. It was while I was lying there among the fresh clean linen and blankets that the Sister stopped and, turning to the accompanying nurse, said, "I don't think I have ever seen anyone enjoying their stay here as this young woman!"

During the day we would watch the orderlies throw huge dollops of polish onto the floor and then buff the lino with a heavy, weighted mop which was swung back and forth until one could literally eat off the floor.

When the chief Medical Officer did his round, he was followed by all the important staff. Matron would wear a white glove and quickly run her finger along ledges and rails in case an orderly had missed a speck of dirt. As this inspection progressed through the ward we had to lie to attention, arms under the sheets, feet together (I have since heard the same story from other service people who spent time in military hospitals). If you were unlucky enough to break a leg or arm and you were strung up to the rails above, of course you couldn't lie to attention.

Whilst staying in bed we were a captive audience for all sorts of visitors, especially the padre, who would seat himself by the bed, ask questions and give comforting words. As we were mostly miles away from our homes and families and so did not get many visitors. We were pleased if someone took the time to talk to us.

Naturally I was worried about myself and lost weight waiting for results and to know what the future held for me. Came the day when there was an earnest discussion between Sister and the MO which I could not overhear. I was not informed of the contents of their talk.

On June 6th our beds were pulled into the middle of the wards for a big spring clean when I was approached by the MO who told me I was being transferred to Brompton Chest Hospital in London and that I was to be escorted by a WAAF Sergeant. I was stunned. Through my mind raced thoughts that I would not be joining my intake for the Passing Out Parade and then on to a posting. I was also now worried sick as to what the medical people thought was wrong with me.

My transfer was put into action and after collecting my clearance chit and travel warrant from the Orderly Room I was escorted to the railway station by a dour-faced sergeant who was not at all pleased to be travelling to London with me. Several hours later, after an uncomfortable journey, we arrived in London and were met by a WVS (Women's Voluntary Service) lady who was to take me to Brompton Hospital.

On arrival at the hospital I was handed over to the Lady Almoner, along with the documents I was given at Wilmslow. The sergeant wished me luck and left to return to Wilmslow.

Brompton Hospital was a very old, established hospital, grey and large. The lady Almoner phoned for someone to pick me up and take me to the ward I was to stay in. It was a two bed ward. The other occupant was a small girl of about nine who appeared angelic but turned out to be a spoilt brat. I was informed that there was a small military wing in the ward above where I was and as I looked outside I saw a fire escape stair and at the top a couple of sailors enjoying the sun.

Once I was settled in to my new ward the tests and x-rays continued. I had to swallow a barium meal, a thick paste, and stand behind a machine with a few medical men watching the barium's progress through my body with an occasional, "There it goes! No... we've lost it again... No, no, it's back again," and so on. I appeared to be causing quite a bit of consternation. From what I remember, Brompton Hospital was either side of a road connected with a dark underground passage. The first time I had to traverse this building I was petrified. There were trolleys along the wall with sputum mugs. There were grey clad, soft-footed nurses gliding along at high speed and patients, some with TB looking pale, their skin stretched across their cheek bones. Being ignorant of the disease I was frightened of catching TB, after all I was breathing the same air and sharing the same sets of cutlery.

The nurse told me I was to have a bronchoscopy; it sounded horrible... and it was. First, a needle was inserted in my throat to deaden it and then I was taken down to theatre, where I was prepared for the bronchoscopy. I was told to open my mouth wide and not to cough. Well we all know what happens when we are told not to do something – we immediately need to do it. What felt like a huge drainpipe was inserted into my mouth and down my throat. I'm not *au fait* with medical terminology, but I do know it was a dreadful experience. I knew the doctors were trying to see what was causing the shadow on the X-ray and therefore did not cough.

On the bright side of things, I was given a 48-hour leave pass to go home after the bronchoscopy. Dressed in my best blue and red tie, shoes polished and buttons gleaming (of course I had packed my Duraglit in with my small kit) I headed for the underground, the Northern Line and on to Finchley. London had not changed in the few months since I left for the WAAF but I had. Now I was used to travelling on my own, I was one of the girls in blue, I was part of the services. It was great to be home, even for a few hours, and what amused me was the comment made by anyone I knew saying "Hello, when do you go back then?" I hadn't even arrived home! Everything appeared small after the big hangers, huts and hospitals, but once home everything fell into place. Of course my parents were worried for me. I had left home looking so fit and without a care in the world until I had had the x-ray.

In the evening I got in touch with Betty my friend who had not joined the services and we made arrangements to meet at the local dancehall and then possibly catch the tube to London. The local dancehall sometimes had a band but more often than not a record player and MC would suffice and we danced to Ted Heath, Glen Miller, Victor Sylvester etc. Looking around the near empty hall the song "What's good is in the Army, What's left will never harm me" sprung to mind. Many of the local lads had been called up or volunteered for the services and some had gone into factories in other parts of the country. There were a few civilians, some airmen and soldiers and also some American GIs.

Slow, slow, quick-quick slow, the foxtrot was danced, and quickstepping and jiving. We had a great time and I made dates I knew I couldn't keep, knowing next that Monday I would be back in Brompton Hospital.

On my return to the hospital I came out of the tube station and was aware of the silence, everything was hushed until there was an earth-shuddering explosion not far from where I was standing. I hadn't realized there was an air raid in progress and that a rocket had exploded.

I continued back to Brompton Hospital, made myself known at the desk and returned to my ward. Returning from taking a shower, I found the doctor sitting by my bed. He looked weary and as he slumped in the chair, he said "Eileen, I believe you do shorthand and typing?"

"Yes," I replied, "but I'm a bit rusty. Haven't done any for months."

"Fine," he said, smiling, "I need someone to take dictation after I've completed an operation and it would be a great help if you could assist me."

From then on, while I was at the hospital, the doctor would come onto the ward and I would struggle to keep up with his reports and findings after surgery, occasionally stopping him to spell out a medical word or term.

I was to have another Barium Meal and x-rays taken. I was standing with Sister in the ward when there was an ear-splitting noise as a V2 rocket plunged into a nearby building and we were thrown against the wall by the blast. The lamp bracket on the wall twisted with the force. The bombing in the neighbourhood of the hospital was getting pretty bad and standby lighting was at the ready in case power was lost, which would be disastrous during an operation.

It was decided that I would be transferred to the military wing of King Edward VII sanatorium in Chichester. Once more it was goodbye to the friends I had made at Brompton. The sailors in the ward above had been in the habit of coming down the fire escape and into the ward, making tea, with permission from the nurse, in a little kitchen off the ward, then we would sit and chat, which helped to pass the time more pleasantly.

The doctors had finally found out what the shadow on the x-ray was all about. I'm not sure of all the details, they were not on my pay book and with all my moves, papers have been lost, but in plain language there was a cyst on or near my lung. I was told it was not dangerous at that stage but in years to come could it be a problem, so they planned to remove it. I was fortunate that one of the Britain's best surgeons was going to perform the surgery at Chichester.

Mum was allowed to accompany me to the sanatorium and so, armed with my small kit bag, gas mask and tin helmet, we made for Victoria Station and our train. The station was milling with service personnel, men and women, all hastily making tracks for their destinations. We found our allotted coach, which had been reserved, on the window in large print was a label saying 'RE-SERVED – SICK WAAF'. I didn't feel sick and I didn't look sick, my cheeks were rosy red, I had eaten far better than I had in civilian life but there I was … and who was I to argue?

The train was filled to capacity. The corridors packed as servicemen and women sat on the floor, stood in the coaches and used every available space. We asked some sailors standing just at our door if they would like to use the empty seats left after we had seated ourselves and of course in a flash they were in, with kitbags and cases thrown up into the luggage racks. They were on their way to Portsmouth and were glad to sit for the journey. Later Mum and I had our lunch of egg and lettuce sandwiches which Mum had prepared. We were fortunate in having a few chickens at the end of our garden and these tiny bantam hens did us proud and produced perfect little eggs each day, although they laid their eggs in all sorts of unusual places, turning their beaks up at the prepared nests. They preferred to use the base of a lilac tree or under the bush for their egg laying.

As we sped on to our destination through suburbs we hadn't seen before, the semi-detached and detached houses which flanked the railway flashed past. Busy scenes in the gardens: a tin bath hanging on the shed wall, someone planting out vegetables – potatoes or sprouts to swell their meagre rations. I saw children playing on top of a buried Anderson shelter which had probably been installed at the very onset of war like our own shelter in the back garden. During the first cold winter, the condensation would run down the sides of the cold steel and soak into our bedding which would be wet and cold by morning. At first we had a mud floor and the dank, earthy smell filled our nostrils and lingered. Forever after, that smell would immediately take me back to the days of the war and that shelter.

As time went by the council put in cement floors with drains and in some cases a wall just in front of the doorway. It was hoped the wall would save the people inside from blast and shrapnel, but in the case of one of our neighbours, a piece of shrapnel ricocheted off the wall and hit a small girl in the chest, lodging in her lung. Next day we were shocked to see her 'siren suit' – the name for the all-in-one warm suit which became popular during the war – hanging on the line with bloodstains on it. It made mockery of the so-called safety wall.

At the first sound of the air raid siren – the wailing Minnie – our dog Flotsam, a 'half-and-halfer' (half Pekinese/half Pomeranian) would rush in front of us to be first into the shelter, followed closely by Peter the cat. Mum would pick up our 'box', which contained birth certificates, insurance policies, wedding certificates etc. and of course we couldn't forget the budgie in its cage. What a sight we must have looked!

This was our 'home' for the duration: homework was done there, meals eaten, books read and of course we slept there, if not soundly, fitfully. We would often hear shrapnel whistling as it came down to earth from an exploded bomb or shell. We had a few near misses and our neighbour would call out, "you alright Mr Smith?" and we would put our heads out of the opening to assure them we were okay.

On one occasion a bomb fell opposite our house and hit a small infant school. The huge crater was still smouldering when we went to investigate and there were toys and books strewn over a large area, the pungent smell of cordite filling our nostrils. Just a fraction of difference when the bomb was released from the German plane and it would have been us that received a direct hit, which would have been fatal in spite of the shelter.

Looking out of the train window I recalled my school years during the war as we sped on towards our destination. We were told to get off at a station near Midhurst and as we alighted an Army corporal came forward to meet us. We were amazed at the organisation which had gone in to my transfer and care taken to see we were met at each stop. As there were a couple of seats in the army car we asked the driver if we could take two extra servicemen on a bit further and he agreed.

Making our way through the beautiful Sussex countryside we saw in the distance the Sanatorium on a hill with green lawns stretching out from it. There was a wing set aside for the military personnel, men and women who had problems associated with lungs and chest. The sanatorium was originally built for the wealthy to recuperate after TB – fresh air and good food for a speedy recovery.

After being admitted at the office Mum and I were taken along the corridors to my room. It was a lovely room with doors opening onto a balcony with views over the lawns and downs. I just could not believe my eyes; it was such a beautiful room and I did not have to share it with anyone. Mum was happy to see me installed there and we said our goodbyes. A taxi was to take her down to a hotel in Midhurst. It would be a good break for her, with my two youngest brothers still at home, she still had to make the rations go as far as possible. She would go miles if she heard rabbit was for sale at a certain shop or extra fish was available from a far-away fishmonger. She would enjoy the rest and change.

As Mum left the ward nurse came in and said, "When you've unpacked your things, make your way to the dining room, Eileen." My things didn't take long to unpack. Into the drawer went one pair of 'pyjamas striped white and blue and fleecy for the use of', underwear 'twilights' and 'blackouts', thick grey stockings, cleaning things for shoes and buttons. Dressing gown on the hook behind the door, Coty lipstick and powder on the dressing table top. These all arranged, I took a look at myself in the mirror, took a deep breath and was ready to meet the other service people in this wing.

The dining room seemed crowded. There were, in fact, about eight other people already seated waiting for dinner to be served. I was introduced by the nurse to the others, who were all male patients, and there was a look of interest as I was the only female on the wing.

There was 'Pilot Officer Prune', I said to myself, about a dashing RAF pilot. He was handsome, debonair, wearing a cravat at the neck of his jacket. There were two Canadian airmen, one a Navigator and one, Don, a DR (dispatch rider), a Polish airman, a Dutch sailor and an army chap – it was a veritable League of Nations.

The table was set with a damask tablecloth, matching serviettes and silver cutlery. The meal was delicious and plenty of it and the conversation flowed between us with jokes and teasing.

During the next few days I was given more x-rays and tests. I was seen by the surgeon and anaesthetist and a date was fixed for my operation. It was now becoming a reality. No more tests; they now knew what had to be done.

In the meantime I was in demand for walks and spent glorious hours walking through the sweet-smelling forest, the pine needles making a soft carpet under our feet.

On returning to the sanatorium, Sister in Charge, who had been worrying about me when she saw me disappear across the lawns with my companions, would call out

"WAAF Smith, where are you going?" she was concerned for my welfare and my virginity – and so was I!

Then it was 'O.D.' – Operation Day. I had been told
the day before, "No breakfast for you, this is your last
meal until after your operation".

It couldn't have been later than 5.00am when I was
woken up by the orderly.

"Here, put these on," she said, pushing some things
into my hands. There was a long pair of thick woolen
socks, a scarf and a cotton gown with ties at the back. I
placed my lucky coin in the left sock, put on the gown
and then placed the scarf on my head *à la* Lana Turner,
the film star. I put a good bit of lipstick on and powdered
my face.

Sister in charge for the day was a neat, trim-waisted,
glamorous woman. She had been particularly nice to me
and I pleaded with her to be with me when going down
to the Operating Theatre.

"Smithy, what on earth are you doing?" She looked
shocked and came toward me with outstretched arms.
"Your hair has to go under the scarf, not a bit showing,
here let me do it… and wipe that lipstick and powder off
your face… think of the germs!"

I had not been thinking of germs, I was thinking about
being slowly wheeled on the trolley, making an exit for
my friends – but sister soon put a stop to that. It was to be
plain Jane and no nonsense. Nevertheless, I did get a good
send off. As I was wheeled out of my room towards the
lift which was to take me to the Operating Theatre the
men lined the corridor and called out, "Good luck
Smithy," "Chop, Chop", "We know what we're having

for dinner", and so on. It cheered me on and I went past them smiling and ready for anything.

As I lay on the trolley, the overhead lights seemed to be rushing down on me and the doors of the corridors crashed as we made our way through them.

Sister left me outside the Operating Theatre and soon I was being told to count backwards from 5. I got as far as three and knew no more…

As if no time had passed I was back in my room and opening my eyes. I saw a nurse sitting at the bedside winding bandages. I asked for water and tried to sit up but there was a lead weight in my chest.

It was over, I had undergone a major operation and had a 13-inch scar on my back, the stitches making it look remarkably like a bone of a large fish.

The following few days entailed series of turning this way and that to get the fluid out of my lungs. Then came the awful day when a brisk nurse, her stiff white starched uniform rustling about her, arrived with a trolley covered with a squeaky-clean cloth under which were hidden some implements of torture, one of which was a long needle and this was inserted into a spot just below my shoulder blade, if I remember rightly. It was a dreadful feeling; like most people, I hate needles. On about the third time I pleaded with the nurse not to do it again and after consultation with Sister it was thankfully decided they had done what was necessary.

Then came a few sessions of physiotherapy to get my arm working again to regain muscle strength; it was harder than I would have imagined to gradually get my arm to lift up above my head. I did manage it but it wasn't, at this stage, straight. 'A good job it isn't my saluting arm,' I remember thinking.

During this time of being confined to bed I was able to use my knowledge of Morse code to tap, very slowly, messages to the chap next door, through the thin wall.

The food was good, much better than I had eaten in years since rationing. It being a hospital, and moreover a Sanatorium, we had fresh eggs (a real treat in wartime Britain), probably donated, and a few other special foods. My room was bedecked with flowers, a huge bouquet of gladioli from the girls at my last job; they were so colourful and really cheered me up.

Finally, I was up and about and told I could join the others in the dining room. I put on some lipstick, brushed my hair and was on my way to the dining room when I was stopped by Sister.

"WAAF Smith, I think you had better go back to your room, get out of your dressing gown and into uniform."

I was not pleased, I didn't want to struggle into stockings, bra, shirt, collar, tie etc as my arm was so stiff, but orders were orders.

Physiotherapy continued and it was decided I should now start walking to get my lungs working properly again, which I did, through the beautiful woods, smelling deliciously of the fir trees as we walked on the carpet of pine needles. What a funny bunch we must have looked from afar. We had all had some kind of surgery on our chests, some on the right side and some on the left and so we listed to either side as we shambled along.

The length of our walks gradually increased until they were long enough to take us to our goal, the lovely old pub at the end of the lane – a small, intimate, low-beamed building set in a cottage garden.

The innkeeper was very good and kept our glasses for us in a special place. (As an aside, I have just broken my glass, which I have kept all these years. It had travelled the length and breadth of Britain, to Scotland, Australia and to the North of Queensland where I now live. It smashed onto a stone floor into a million tiny glass beads. I have never seen anything like it. I was saddened by the break-age – that glass contained a whole lifetime of memories.)

We did enjoy our drink in such a cosy atmosphere and looked forward to the next day's exercise but … the Doctor called us all into his room. We wondered what it was all about as he stood, a little man, his thin lips tightly drawn across his teeth, almost on tiptoe in order to look into our eyes.

"Now, it has come to my hearing that you have been frequenting a public house just outside these grounds, is this so?"

Of course we were not going to deny it and said, "Yes, we went for a drink during our exercise."

"This has got to stop!" the Doctor said firmly, glaring at us and pacing along our small line. "This just won't do!"

We were stunned. We couldn't see what harm a drink could do. Why was he was so angry?

"What we will do…" the Doctor said, "is to allow you a drink or wine in the dining room with your dinner. It will be rationed, of course."

We thanked him and agreed it was fair, but at the same time it didn't take the place of a goal to make for whilst exercising … and what a goal!

So, it was to be beer at the dining table. I was not at all keen on beer, although I did like shandy, and so I did a swap, my beer for an ice cream – fair exchange. At that time I was quite happy with the arrangement. But we did miss the walk and the banter as we made our way to the 'winning post'.

Looking back now, I really can't believe how blasé I was about the whole thing. Today with all the backup, visiting hours and follow-up checks after a big operation there is the feeling of cosseting, but then, in my 19th year, I just coped on my own. No visitors during my stay at Midhurst and then, on returning to Wilmslow several days later, just a cursory look at the scar by the MO and, "Okay, Smith, you can do light duties until you are posted." And that was that.

After physiotherapy and exercises, my left arm gradually became stronger. The luxury of the Sanatorium was not lost on me and I had enjoyed the super walks around the area. One of the Canadian soldiers, Don, and I would take walks to the woods and onto a small incline, where we could look over the Sussex scenery. He was a farming boy and he a DR (dispatch rider) on his trusty motorbike. Apparently during rifle practice one of his fellow soldiers had accidentally pulled the trigger whilst pointing the gun at Don and a bullet hit him in the chest and went right through his back, missing all the vital organs by a fraction of an inch.

We spent hours talking about our respective child-hoods. He came from Manitoba and strangely, as a child I too had lived in Canada. Dad had been in the First World War and on demob, soon after marrying and with two children, he took the opportunity of emigrating to Canada and we sailed from Liverpool when I was just 11 months old. Ex-servicemen were given a parcel of land of about 160 acres, a 'quarter section', I think it was called. The Canadian government provided a brand new shed, a few cows, a couple of horses and a few other agricultural pieces of equipment.

We were in a place called Red Deer, between Calgary and Edmonton. Mum was only about 21 at the time, a townie from Finchley, a suburb of London, and not a very strapping young lady at that, prone to fainting in the classroom as she grew tall and lanky – but in the four years we were there she not only raised my brother Den and myself, but also had another baby and one on the way. She cooked all her own bread and cakes, bottled fruits and vegetables, helped with calving, rode the horse bareback, helped slaughter pigs and chickens and all-in-all was a perfect farmer's wife. Remember too, that she had no way of phoning her mum when things got tough! It was 40° below zero in the winter and she had to melt snow to get drinking water when the well and pump froze. She told me that if the fire was almost out by morning she would faint with the extreme cold.

Dad meanwhile had felled trees in the wood to make room for some wheat and other crops. He had sheep, which the wolves helped themselves to and the cows, on arrival, had been so thin and weedy that I was laughingly told that Mum had to prop them up when milking them!

Mary, a horse with a white flash on her nose, was a clever horse; she had learnt how to pull the stable door bolt with her teeth and would get out. On one occasion she managed to get herself into the river which ran through the farm at a time when the ice was thick in some places and thin in others. Mary was soon in trouble and Dad went out after her, getting frostbitten in the heels for his efforts. I believe that was almost the last straw, when he decided to go back to England. Meanwhile Den and I had a life of absolute freedom.

I returned to the farm in later life and stood on the very ground we played on. It was a beautiful area, I think it was called Poplar Ridge. We were on a hill which, as a child, I thought was a mountain. We used to go down it on trays when it snowed. There was a river running through the land and the CPR (Canadian Pacific Railway) also had tracks through it and there was a viaduct; not a lot of the 160 acres was really available to farm.

I didn't know Don's area, but loved to hear all about his childhood. He was almost ready to leave the sanatorium and when he did we vowed to meet again, although we never did. But we did leave a lasting sign of us having been there, ES and DB entwined initials in the bark of an old tree overlooking the valley. I continued to have my exercise walks with some of the other men and the days passed quickly.

Among these men was a Polish Air Force man who was a little older than the rest of us. He had baled out into the North Sea after his aircraft had been hit and had spent time in the freezing water until he could be rescued; as a consequence he developed lung troubles. He was charming but not particularly good looking. Somehow my woman's instinct told me to beware, especially when he asked me to go for a walk. The reason for my being wary was, one day while standing by a window overlooking the manicured lawns, he suddenly made a movement and he grabbed my blue serge covered bosom, saying in his thick broken English "You know, I think you're lovely, I want you but I don't want just the lick of the ice cream, I want the whole cornet."

Well! Apart from having my bosom gripped in a vice-like hold, once I realized what had happened I saw the funny side of it. It had to be the funniest line I had ever heard but when I laughed my would-be lover looked hurt and then angry, muttering that he didn't understand these English girls, they were cold-hearted. I suppose in a strange way it was a compliment, although one far removed from the one I received while rowing on the Thames with the shy young man I met while "Giving a Hand on the Land". This Polish airman was giving a hand where he thought it would be best placed!

Also among us 'walking wounded' was Snowy, another Canadian Airman. He was tall, fair, good-looking and had one very big phobia; he was frightened of bats. At King Edward VII Sanatorium we didn't have the normal doors to our rooms, they were louvered half doors – fresh air and all that – but according to him, the bats could come in and suck at his toes. Snowy was petrified and went to all sorts of lengths to make sure his feet were not exposed to the nocturnal threat of these bloodsucking monsters.

On Sundays we were expected to attend a church service with all the other patients and we assembled in the church, which had been built especially for the particular type of patients who would be attending the service. There was plenty of fresh air because there was an open roof and as a result, one could lift ones eyes to the heavens whilst the service was in progress, watching the puffs of white clouds as they slowly drifted across the church.

Finally, I was given an examination by the head doctor who pronounced me fit enough to have a spot of leave and return to Wilmslow. So I said goodbye to my fellow servicemen and to the wonderful nurses who had looked after me. I was collected from the Sanatorium by a WAAF driver in a small jeep. She had orders to deliver me to the picket post at RAF Tangmere.

We enjoyed the drive back through the lovely countryside and over the hill and into the gates of the fighter station Tangmere. What a thrill it was for me to be here at this very famous Battle of Britain station. I felt in awe of it all. I presented myself at the picket post along with my papers and was given instructions as to where I would find my bed for the night before proceeding to London.

As it was only a few days since my major operation, I was finding my case, tin helmet and gas mask together with small kit very heavy and my arms were aching. The stitches had been taken out but the arm was still weak and so was I. I found the house, found an empty room, made up the bed with the sheets I had been given and went in search of a meal...

Tangmere was a small village. I walked the length of the road and was directed to the Mess. I was wearing the tie given to service people when on sick leave. It was red and very noticeable, but nobody too the slightest bit of interest in this skinny, pale-looking WAAF. I found an empty place and sat down to eat the meal.

Returning to the house, I undressed and got into the hard, cold bed. After an hour I woke up shivering. The bedding felt damp; it probably hadn't had an airing in weeks. I sat up, feeling stiff and cold. My arm and shoulder were aching and I made an effort to make the bed a bit more comfortable. There was a musty smell about the place and I felt miserable and alone.

For the past couple of weeks I had been eating lovely, well-presented, appetizing meals and sleeping in crisp, white linen and here I was, after undergoing major surgery, lying in a damp bed with thick twill sheets and rough grey blankets. I was so happy to see the morning sky becoming streaked with a red blush and then the blue with the sun breaking through.

After a hot bath I once more made my way to the mess and had a delicious meal of fried egg on a piece of fried bread – oh, those lovely calories! The egg was the usual white rubber with a little hard ball of yolk in the middle but it was great and I polished it off with a hot cup of tea.

Returning to the house, I collected my belongings and made my way along the street to the Orderly Room. I was amazed and very relieved to find a travel warrant and other necessary papers on a clip in the office.

I caught a shuttle bus to a nearby railway station and was on my way home for ten days sick leave before journeying to Wilmslow. I was looking forward to going home for a bit of pampering. I was also looking forward to seeing my friends in Civvy Street.

As before, the train was packed to the roof with service personnel. There was very little room in the compartments and kitbags and cases were everywhere. Their owners were sitting and standing in the corridors, whiling away the hours smoking, talking, playing cards etc.

At last I heard the words, "Next Stop Victoria Station". I collected my belongings and moved through the throng of people to the gates, showing my travel warrant to the guard. Then I was on my way to the underground station, looking for the Northern Line and Finchley, about 11 miles from London.

I reached the top of the stairway which led down into the depths of the subway. All I could see was a sea of faces as they hurried up and out into the fresh air. My case and gas mask were getting heavy and as I contemplated kicking some of my gear down the stairs a soldier noted my red tie and came to my rescue. Without a word he picked up the case and small kit, taking them all the way to my platform. I was so grateful and couldn't thank him enough.

It had been a long day; I was beginning to flag and realized that I wasn't as fit as I thought I was. Once the train emerged from the dark tunnels into the fresh air I knew I was nearing Finchley. I walked along Squires Lane, a little uphill, or so it seemed to me, and knocked at the door. It was opened by Dad. I was near to crying as I stepped into the hall. Dad was shocked to see my apparent distress and was all for immediately phoning the Air Ministry for not looking after me at this end of the journey, but I persuaded him to do nothing of the sort, as I was anxious to get on with my WAAF career and did not want anything further to stop me.

I got in touch with my friend Betty and we arranged to go to the local *Palais de Dance*. It was nice to get into something feminine again, although I didn't mind the uniform, in fact I felt smart and trim in my light blue/grey WAAF uniform. As we entered the hollow-sounding hall, there were strains of Victor Sylvester playing a foxtrot. Today being a Saturday there was no band, just a record player.

We looked around the sparsely-filled dance hall but saw very few young men, just a few servicemen on leave like myself and a couple of American GIs. As the next record was placed on the turntable, the MC called out over the microphone, "everybody take their partners for a quick-step."

I felt a tap on my shoulder and a voice said "May I have this dance Ma'am," and looking up I saw one of the Americans at my side. He was a sweet-smelling, gum-chewing soldier and once on the floor he held my hand while I danced rings around him as he swayed his fat little behind in time to the music.

We had a great time that evening but I was aware of my arm and had to tell the GI that I was, in fact, in the WAAF and on sick leave, for which I got a "you don't say ma'am" nevertheless we had a few more dances and he, along with his friend, who had been dancing with Betty, walked with us to our bus-stop. As we waited under the tiny street lamp I heard Betty give her infectious giggle and this smooth drawling voice saying, "No, you're not fat, you're just pleasingly plump." What a line!

It was 1944, war had been waging for four years, London was milling with servicemen and women from all corners of the globe. Hammersmith Palais and the Stage Door were but a couple of meeting places. I went with a friend to the Stage Door Canteen and it was great to stand with other jazz fans listening to a small group of musicians playing all the latest tunes. We danced, had a drink, then strolled around London. Not the London we had known before the war, but still a hub of activity and excitement, especially to those men and women who had come from overseas and were visiting the Old Country for the first time.

The dance halls were packed and there was no room to show off and execute the finer steps of the dance, we just moved around slowly in time to the music with the little darting lights from the glistening mirror-ball above us playing on our faces. There were people standing on all sides of the ballroom 'eyeing-up the talent' and deciding which girl or boy to ask for the next rumba or tango.

I recall, before I joined the WAAF making the mistake of going to a local dance with Gwen. I had been told I was pretty, but next to Gwen… no. Gwen was beautiful, with thickly-lashed green eyes and soft, curly, strawberry blonde hair. She was a model, and her luminous eyes looked out from professional photographs in her home.

At the dance we sat alongside the dance floor and as we chatted, on more than one occasion, a handsome officer would come towards us and I would get ready to accept his offer to dance … but he would make a bee-line for

Gwen, leaving me sitting there, blushing furiously, feeling very much a wallflower.

At these dances, before and after the war, friendships were often made, but nothing of the lasting nature; we would most probably never meet again. In those years there were so many hellos and goodbyes and even today I find it quite easy to say goodbye to people, knowing that in all likelihood our paths will never cross again, content to remain just 'ships that pass in the night'.

The film *Gone with the Wind* was showing at the local cinema and we queued for hours to get in, finally settling into the deep chairs with an expectant air. The film was a long one, long enough to have an interval and I lost myself in the action completely. I admired headstrong Scarlet, swooned at Rhett Butler's good looks and felt for the shy and good Melanie. All too soon it was over and we were making our bleary-eyed way out of the cinema into the clear bright outdoors. It had been a wonderful film and one which never lost its lustre. It would be shown to millions, even 50 years hence.

I had enjoyed my sick leave and was getting fitter every day but it was coming to an end and I was ready to pick up the threads of service life. I packed my small kit, polished my shoes, pressed my shirt, put on my crisp, starched collar and said my goodbyes once again.

I didn't like leaving Mum, she looked so tiny and lonely standing by the door waving to me. Out of her five children, three of us were in the services. Brother Den was in the Air Force, Bill was in the Navy and I, of course, was in the WAAF. When I had told him I wanted to join the WAAF Den had said, "You don't want to do that. The girls are common. You won't like it." But of course I took no notice.

Bill was stationed in Northern Ireland and was having a ball. He was in Safety Equipment. He had always been quiet and shy, but in a few months he became much more self-assured. He told me he had met an older WREN and I said, "She's probably after your money Bill." His reply was, "Not my money!"

When we were both in London on leave we would accompany each other to a film or a dance if we hadn't a partner. On one occasion we decided to go to a Lyons Corner House for a meal. Sitting at our table, soft lights, soft music, plush carpets, tablecloths and flowers on the table it made it very special after the mess halls we had both been used to. Although the meals were reasonably priced there was a feeling of opulence created by Lyons.

As we sat enjoying the meal, one of the musicians, playing a soulful, gypsy love-song and dressed in gypsy garb came gliding toward our table. 'Manuel' proceeded to sigh and grin as he played his romantic tune to the 'lovers', while Bill and I sat, embarrassed, but not liking to spoil the illusion for our would-be little cupid.

After the meal we strolled along the London streets, looking into the windows which were now sparingly stocked with goods. We were going to a dance and Bill needed some "Dutch courage" in the shape of a couple of beers before he felt he could summon the nerve to ask a girl to dance or even to execute the steps. Bill was very handsome in his naval uniform and would find no problems in getting a partner to dance with him.

As I waved Mum goodbye, Dad accompanied me to the station and wanted to introduce me to his friends at his favourite local pub. They asked questions, some of them a bit too searching about what was going on in the Air Force, although of course at this stage I knew nothing but I looked very secretive and said, "Sorry, not allowed to say anything." I downed the drink Dad had bought me and it made my eyes water. I was still a lemonade girl for the moment.

After more goodbyes I boarded the train to London and found my train for Manchester with the help of the RTO. There was the usual delay as a red-capped SP (Special Policeman) stopped me and requested to see my identity card, travel warrant etc. These SPs had an uncanny knack of stopping servicemen and women who were rushing to catch their train or bus. They would peruse your documents achingly slowly, before grudgingly saying, "Off you go, you'll miss your train," which in all probability you had done, thanks to them!

Once more I was on the train bound for Wilmslow, but this time I was on my own, no charges to look after, no worries about "what it would be like". I knew, and I also knew I had missed the Passing Out Parade after the month's training. I had missed seeing the friends I had made and I had missed training for the Special Duties I had been earmarked for. Now, a few weeks after my first arrival at the WAAF camp, I was on my way back again to await a posting.

Arriving in Manchester I made my way to Wilmslow, and presented myself to the Picket Post, handing in the paperwork I had been given at Tangmere. The orderly gave me the usual sheets, pillow case, packet of sanitary towels (for the use of) and then the hut number I was to go to while waiting for my posting.

First thing was to report to the MO (medical officer) and he gave me a cursory examination, remarking on my very neat fishtail scar. He was very impressed when I told him the name of the surgeon who had operated on me, Mr Price Thomas, but not as impressed as I was when he told me that he was no less than King George VI's own surgeon who was helping the war effort by operating on military personnel. I was lucky! The MO then wrote out a chit saying I was to be on light duties for two weeks.

Leaving my kit on the wire base of an unmade bed in hut 11, I went in search of the holding hut, where my kitbag had been deposited before I left for London and Brompton Hospital. 2170298 Smith's kitbag was under a huge stack of gear. I pulled it out and lugged it back to my hut. What a terrible mess there was inside the bag. My greatcoat, which had been stiff and smooth, was now like a rag and I heartily wished I had taken more care to fold it. My best blue (second tunic) was also crumpled like a rag, as was the skirt. Then came my shoes, which had been slightly worn in and were beginning to have that worn and polished look but were now dented and mouldy-looking.

I spent the rest of the day ironing, polishing and making myself presentable for the officer in charge of my duties. Ironing was achieved by using a communal iron and I was the proud possessor of the sweetest travel iron (I still have it). It is pale blue with a little stand. The plug can still be plugged into a light socket and it did a sturdy job throughout my WAAF days, busily ironing a shirt or skirt for a parade or for a date.

Now looking smart in my newly-pressed clothes and polished shoes and buttons I presented myself to the Orderly Room, whereupon I was told my duties were to be in the camp canteen. This was going to be a completely new experience for me but it didn't appear to be too hard or too difficult. I was instructed to work with another girl making sandwiches and was sent to a table where there were huge bowls containing various fillings for the sandwiches: spam, cheese and jam. The spam was chopped in a mincer, as was the cheese and the jam was watered down "for easy spreading".

Spam was one of my favourite things (still is). When I was the junior Secretary at Davis Tyres in Cricklewood my daily job was to go to the workman's shed next to our building and buy snacks. The mouthwatering slices of Spam were fried and placed between a crisp roll. I was as thin as a rake and no amount of these delicious rolls put an ounce on me. So here in the camp I ate some of the perks of the job – a nibble here, a nibble there – until in a few days I noticed the buttons on my tunic were beginning to pull a little…

The days went well. We had lectures to attend again and one day we were told there was to be a Route March. Although my arm was getting more like its old self, I still couldn't use it as well as before and so took a little longer fixing buttons etc., picking up heavy items and so.

"Come along Smith! We can't wait all day. Tallest on the right, shortest on the left."

We shuffled into straight lines and were ready for the order. "By the left… quick march!" followed, as we moved forward, by "left, right, left, right… come on lift those arms… keep in step…"

And so we marched out of the gates and into the leafy lanes and through the village and the little cottages and shops. We marched in step, enjoying the change of scene, the sunshine and the exercise. It was a long march and on returning to camp, as the old saying goes, we were 'walking on our cap badges'. As we neared the gates the corporal shouted, "Come on girls! Lift those arms! Don't slouch!"

I was feeling very weary by now and on arriving back at the hut collapsed onto the wire bed. I should have spoken up at the onset of the march - I was only on light duties, but at the time I felt great.

It was 'sports afternoon' and that meant we were allowed off camp, but we would use the time to do anything but sport! I had had a week of sandwich-making, marching and lectures and was ready for a change of scene.

Unlike the girls of my first intake, who had been confined to barracks on suspicion of stealing sink plugs, there was no such problem now and so, I, along with some of the other girls from the hut now made for the bus to take us to the "big smoke" – Manchester – to see the sights and to "paint the town red!"

We looked smart, buttons highly polished, belt buckles glinting in the sun, shoes gleaming with spit and polish, stockings thick grey Lyle with their seams straight. My shoulder bag, navy blue with shoulder strap, was on my left shoulder, leaving my right arm free for saluting "longest way up shortest way down" and we were off…

"Just a moment you gals!"

We turned and saw, emerging from the picket post, a WAAF Officer.

"I want some volunteers…" I heard her say.

I had heard all the stories of how volunteers were had. "You there, the tall girl…"

"That's me," I thought.

"… and you there, the one with the fair hair… Come here."

We looked at each other. It looked like our bus would have to go without us and so we told the other girls we would meet up at a certain spot, if possible, later.

"I have a job for you. Climb onto that lorry and when the driver stops at the ablutions, get the sanitary pails, load them onto the lorry and at the incinerator, burn them."

What else could we do but salute and say, "Yes, Ma'am," even though we felt hard-done-by and resentful. We were all dolled up in our best blue, it was our half day off but … orders were orders.

Manchester was like any other big city, old and sooty. We didn't take long to find the shops. The cake shops were empty, with doilies on clean shelves, a reminder of the dainty cakes which had taken pride of place in those windows pre-war. We looked at the latest fashions in the windows – wide, military-style suits and coats although some of the dresses had soft shoulders with a little less padding.

As we walked we sniffed the air and found the fish and chip shop, joining the queue with other service personnel and civilians. Later, we walked along the path, enjoying the hot, steamy chips soaked in salt and vinegar and the anonymity our uniform gave us. Never had fish and chips tasted so good, the smell of the newspaper wrapping enhancing it.

5. RAF East Kirkby

"298 Smith, you're posted. Report to the Orderly Room," the Corporal shouted across the kitchen.

This was it, after all the weeks of tests, hospitals, etc. I was at last being sent on active duty.

"07.30 tomorrow Smith, posting to 5 Group, East Kirkby - that's Bomber Command in Lincolnshire."

This was my first real posting and it was to an operational station. At this stage I was not aware of what my duties at East Kirkby would be, but I do know that if I hadn't had the misfortune to have that x-ray and the subsequent operation, I would have probably have gone with other Clerks Special Duties for training in plotting, ciphering etc... But at least I hadn't been given a discharge…

I went back to the hut, collected a clearance chit and made the rounds of all the necessary offices to get clearance signatures. I returned to my hut and after the corporal had given my kit an inspection as it lay on display on my bed, I packed most of it into my kitbag.

I was getting quite excited but a little apprehensive at the thought of going off on my own into the unknown. After a hurried breakfast and cup of tea I made my way to the bus, which was standing outside the WAAF gates waiting for us to board. We were driven along country lanes to the railway station. My destination in Lincolnshire was Stickney railway station. I had never heard of it and I don't suppose many people had before the war, but I now knew that it was the nearest station to East Kirkby.

Looking around the compartment I saw another WAAF and guessed her to be about 26. Her uniform looked as though it had seen service and was not bright blue like mine, her hat peak was bent right forward over her eyes and her hair was swept up and tucked into a band of the hat. She was very much an 'old stager' who had been in for years, probably since 1939 or '40.

"This your first posting?" she asked. Her smile seemed to say it all – that I looked a very raw recruit – and of course she was right. She said her name was Ruth and her trade had been as a Balloon Operator. She seemed to know all the ropes and all the angles. As we talked, I warmed to her; she was very friendly and as we approached Stickney she helped me with my kit, gas mask and other bits and pieces.

There were several RAF and WAAF personnel alighting and we stood on the lonely, rain-swept station, wondering what we were doing in this dreary-looking neck of the woods. We heard the sound of a lorry coming towards us. "Anyone for East Kirkby?" shouted the driver, and we dashed out into the rain and scrambled up into the back of the lorry, sitting on benches, crowded together and hanging on to whatever we could as the lorry sped along winding country lanes.

We peered out into the wet night but there were no landmarks, just flat farmland with a small dark shape of a building here and there. During World War II, this part of Lincolnshire was dotted with Bomber Command stations and it was not long before I began to learn many of their names. The lorry slowed as we reach 'E.K.'

"Okay, down you get, RAF picket post over there and WAAF over there," he said, pointing vaguely into the dark, wet night. It was now 7 o'clock in the evening, we had been on the move since 07.30 hours and were tired, hungry and I for one was feeling very nervous and apprehensive. The lights of the picket post could be seen through the drizzle and we entered the small room to see the orderly officer in charge. We offered our papers and were told which huts to move into and given sheets, pillow cases and the usual packet of sanitary towels.

I was going into a hut comprising mostly girls from Signals and my new-found friend was given another hut number. She would not be following her own trade of Balloon Operator, but probably something similar.

I made my way towards my hut, which showed a very faint glimmer from its windows and was feeling very sorry for myself. I stumbled and dropped my sheets in the rain, trying to keep my kitbag, tin helmet etc dry. Huge tears rolled down my cheeks. It wasn't fair, I told myself, why couldn't I have been posted with Squibs, Margaret and all the rest of my intake? Why was I left behind? I pushed open the hut door and all eyes turned towards me.

"I've been posted here," I muttered.

"Right," said the girl nearest the door, "there's a spare bed there, if you like." She pointed to an empty bed frame between two made-up beds.

I unpacked my personal things, placing some on my portion of the shared chest of drawers between my bed and the next, hung my gas cape up on the wall hook above the bed and placed my best blue, overcoat etc on hangers, making the cape like a cupboard. My gas mask was placed on the shelf above. Blackouts and twilights (knickers) stockings, bras, etc I placed in my drawers.

The girls in the hut appeared to be very friendly and at once I felt at home. It was great getting settled, having my own bed to sleep on and now I was being taken to the NAAFI as soon as I was ready.

Next morning was spent in of obtaining signatures for my Arrival Chit, getting to know where the various offices and areas were, and having a 'secrecy lecture' – especially important as this was an operational station. As I walked from one place to another, some over fields and others along lanes, I could hear the low rumble of aircraft revving up.

I was to work in the Signals office, which was in the Base HQ. Blondie, one of the girls in the office, was moving to another area. I believe she was a W/OP (wireless operator) and I was replacing her. She was small and a little on the plump side, with short, very blond curls and two little false front teeth, which showed as she grinned, which she did often, her bright blue eyes shining wickedly. I met her as I entered the tomb-like building. There were no windows; light was from overhead light-ing and fresh air was through ducts which ran along the ceilings. The building housed many offices, including some R/T work. I could hear the voices of Waafs as they talked to the aircrews, saw other girls with earphones, listening to Morse code and heard the teleprinter rattling away in the corner. This was the hub of the station and it was awe-inspiring to me, still a very new 'sprog'.

Blondie opened the door of a small office which housed two desks, one larger than the other and at the larger one sat an officer with dark hair, brown eyes and two rings on his sleeve.

The officer looked up from his papers and seeing me said to Blondie, "Hello, who have we here?"

"WAAF Smith Sir," said Blondie.

I stepped forward.

"Welcome aboard. I'm Flight Lieutenant Scott and I hope we can make a good team here. Blondie will show you the ropes."

For the next few days I was shown what my duties would be: a sort of personal assistant to the Station Signals Officer. Some of the work would be preparing call-signs etc for the crews, to be handed out prior to an operation. Of course, it goes without saying, that it had to be 100% accurate and secret. It wasn't hard, but slip-ups on any such work could endanger the lives of the aircrews.

Once these were typed for the day, they were checked and double-checked and then run off on an antiquated Gestetner. There were two satellite stations – Strubby and Spilsby, both a few miles from East Kirkby and so there were a good number of call-signs to organise.

Next to our office was the telephone exchange and I would frequently hear spoken what I took to be the words "rubber knees" before realising that it was, in fact, "number please".

By the time of my arrival, EK has been involved for some time in sending aircraft on night raids, so often when we were lying in bed these huge craft could be heard revving up, soon to take-off and pass overhead, the deafening noise and vibrations making it seem that they were flying within a few feet of the hut. The noise would gradually fade into the distance, each of us saying a silent prayer for the aircrews to return home safely. Those who had aircrew boyfriends would wait with dry mouths and beating hearts until they heard that all had returned, which hopefully was the case.

East Kirkby was a lush farming area and we would walk through the fields to our various posts of duty. The long runways would score across the acres to dispersal centres.

Nearby was Revesby Manor and where a deer herd could be seen, their soft limpid eyes looking trustingly as we passed on foot or on a bike. I could never understand how hunters, could, for their own egotistical satisfaction, bring themselves to shoot such beautiful creatures just to have their heads mounted on a wall.

Also in the area there was a windmill, Bolingbroke Mill, which was a landmark not only for us but also for the aircrews – a sign that they were 'almost home'.

Up on the hill was the radar van and the sort of men who manned her seemed to be 'boffin' types. They always seemed to be a bit untidy – that is, until they were told to present themselves for the morning parade. It must have been a bit lonely up there, cut off from the rest of the camp, but I suppose it did have its advantages…

As I said, the station was far flung and to get to the cook house and many of the other sites meant a long, long walk. I realised that a bicycle would be very useful and became the proud owner of '298 bike', on which I was soon was pedalling along the leafy lanes.

A skirt was not the best apparel to wear in this environment, especially on a bike, so I requested permission to wear more suitable garb, i.e. battledress. This uniform was a delight to wear: the jacket had a hidden panel and buttoned up, the slacks had a side plaquet and buttoned on to the jacket. The jacket was useful for all sorts of things – one in particular was for carrying cakes etc if we could scrounge them from the cookhouse to go with our morning tea.

While sitting in the mess on my first day, I lifted my eyes from my greasy plate and to my surprise, saw the most beautiful paintings on the ceiling. In various hues of blue were diaphanously draped nymphs curled over a blue moon, adding a bit of culture to the surroundings. The paintings were to remain for some years. It is not certain who painted them, but I was told that it was an Italian prisoner of war.

Getting to the mess in winter was tricky as the roads became ridged with hard, icy ruts and the wheels of our bikes would go from one rut to another, often throwing the rider into the hedge to arrive at the mess bruised, wet and hungry. We would throw our bikes in a pile and enter the warm, noisy mess. There was always plenty to eat, more than we had had for the years in civvy street prior to joining up. After the meal it became a practice to make our way to the NAAFI and spend some of our small income on a cup of coffee or tea, or if you felt flush, a custard tart.

There was also the 'Toc-H', which was housed in the village hall, where one could get a cup of tea and, for us Waafs, some extra milk.

As winter got under way, life became very uncomfortable in the huts. It was difficult to keep warm. Many of the windows had broken or cracked panes and no one had the time or the inclination to fix them.

On one occasion I asked an officer if we could have the windows fixed and she gave me a haughty look and said "Bung a piece of rag in it Smith." The snow would blow in through the windows and onto our beds; in the mornings we would find a dusting of snow on our blankets. On occasions, after a heavy rain, the water would come into the hut and we would have to set to with a broom and sweep down the steps. If you were unfortunate enough to be sick with a cold it was well-nigh impossible to get warm.

It was also hard to get washing dry. There was a laundry on camp and usually pyjamas were sent there, but bits of underwear, stockings and shirts were washed in the ablutions and hung on makeshift lines among the trees. The lines became a dangerous obstacle to avoid when going to the toilets at night or returning from a dance or a date after dark. There was a very real possibility of garrotting oneself! Kit inspections often necessitated grabbing our things off the lines and pushing them into our kitbags, often wet and damp, and probably putting the damp articles on the following day - could rheumatism in old age be the result of such practices? But in those far-off days we were more concerned with not being 'put on a charge' than we were for our future well-being, and old age seemed an impossibly distant prospect.

Our shirts had separate collars and many of us took the opportunity of sending these collars to the Chinese

Laundry. They would come back stiff and shiny, with a razor-sharp neck edge. Many a tussle would ensue in an effort to get these springy collars attached to our shirts with a collar stud - a museum piece today. It wasn't hard to recognise the WAAF 'trade mark' – we all had a dull round mark on our throats where the collar stud had pressed!

The huts were heated with coal-fired stoves placed at either end of the hut, and these would become the centre of all activities. We would heat water for a cup of tea or cocoa, toast bread, or heat up some soup and sit chatting or writing letters, balancing the paper on our knees which would be scorched whilst our backs were freezing.

Coke was used to fire these stoves and it was pretty lethal. If the windows were not kept open at night, in the morning the air would be thick with rancid fumes.

During autumn we became quite careless with the ration of fuel and would throw the used coke outside beside the hut, but later, when it became bitterly cold and there was no more fuel ration, we would don our gloves and scarves and go foraging among the old cinders for anything likely to give off a little more heat.

On the WAAF site there was a coke compound surrounded by a high wall and we considered getting into this compound and helping ourselves to extra rations. When the time was ripe, as my arm was still on the weak side, it was decided that I should sit on top of the wall and act as a lookout. With difficulty, I climbed on top of the wall and watched as the remainder of the girls, armed with buckets and shovels, quietly filled them with coke. As I watched from my vantage point I saw in the distance what looked like a torch beam sending shafts of light skywards as the person holding it walked with a swift stride.

"Quick,'" I hissed, "someone's coming!"

We tried to scramble over the wall, but not quite in time. I, for one, couldn't get down quickly, my arm wouldn't take my weight and as the torch searched for culprits there came a loud voice.

"What are you doing?" bawled the WAAF Officer as she shone the light into our faces. "Get down at once! At 08.30 hours you will report here to me." And with that she marched off indignantly and we in turn were furious at being caught.

We assembled at 08.30 hours, standing to attention while the WAAF officer of the day, attended by a Sergeant, walked up and down, her gloved hands clasped behind her back.

"You have all been guilty of what is tantamount to mutiny and if you had been men you would most certainly have been up for Court Martial." She glowered at us and went on. "Let this be a warning to you that there is to be no more stealing. It is unforgivable. There is a war on." As she finished she gave a final disdainful look, detailing the sergeant to dismiss us.

If we couldn't help ourselves to coke we had to find other means of keeping warm. Any old piece of furniture, old broom handles and the backs of wardrobes were broken into pieces to keep us from freezing. Somehow we felt justified in this action as it seemed to us that there was plenty of fuel out there in the coal compound.

Food was not supposed to be taken back to the huts but some Waafs worked in jobs which gave them the opportunity of bringing back left-overs for supper.

One duty which befell some of us was to be on Early Morning Wake Up. If a Waaf needed an early call, it was listed and then the duty girls would go from hut to hut in the cold dark hours of the morning, stumbling through the huts and finding the girl to be woken. Sometimes we would get a rude blast as the girl put her head under the blankets and growled "bloody well buzz off" or words to that effect, but another shake and she would sit up miserably, thanking us whilst throwing the blankets off.

The huts often had a distinct smell of food when one entered and we hoped the duty officer didn't have as good a nose as we did.

The winter conditions also made the ablutions a hazard. Condensation from the pipes dripped down onto the floor and froze over. Pipes and cisterns needed to be thawed out and braziers were kept glowing day and night, sending out rancid fumes. On one occasion I left the office in a hurry, making for the toilet block. Some were out of order and as I dashed from one door to another, unbuttoning my tunic from the battle dress trousers as I went, I pushed open a door, slipped on the icy floor, crashed my head on the toilet and ended up lying spread-eagled among the pipes.

Operations continued all through the winter and when the airfield was blanketed with snow all hands were needed to clear the runways with shovels.

Meanwhile I was doing my little bit, typing, checking and distributing the figures and call-signs prior to a raid. I had become adept at typing figures, knowing that if I hit an incorrect key any mistake on my part would cause problems for the aircrews or the control tower.

Once the day's call-signs were prepared, the stencil sheet was run off ready for distribution and placed in a safe place, to be destroyed at a later date. From time to time I and one other person would go out into the field where a sawn off oil drum made into an incinerator would be filled with top-secret papers. As we stoked the fire, tiny fragments would curl their way skywards, lifted into the light air. In those days there didn't appear to be such a thing as a shredder and even if there was we didn't have one at our disposal and therefore were obliged to use this somewhat archaic but nevertheless very effective method.

Flight Lieutenant Scott – Scotty – and I were seeing a lot of each other outside working hours. I felt he was not looking for any permanent relationship and therefore continued to hide my feelings for him and kept to the banter and witty repartee. We joined in with other groups cycling round the peri track to the local pub, which, like most of the pubs in this area was always packed to overflowing with servicemen and women along with the locals.

It was an atmosphere charged with many conflicting emotions. There would be laughing and joking, the laughter often hiding a deep hurt for friends who had been shot down in action or concern for colleagues who at that very moment were in the cramped confines of a Lancaster, heading for their target for the night. There would usually be a game of darts in progress and I was fairly good at darts so my partner and I could hold our own on the board. A piano would often be softly playing in the background and in the dark corners and quieter places, couples would sit and talk, maybe hopeful that one day they could lead a normal life, but for the moment enjoying their time together and making plans.

Apart from the local pubs, Boston was a rendezvous for dozens of buses and trucks. In the town square, out would spill men and women in various shades of blue, some making for the church hall where they would receive not only religious benefit but also tea and cakes served up by willing workers. Others would make their way to one of the many pubs or to one of the dance halls or cafés and restaurants for a meal.

One café in particular always had a long, snake-like queue, wending its way along the path and up the stairs. Here one could buy sausage, chips and egg for a shilling. To us it was nectar of the gods and we would sit happily in the small, crowded café enjoying fat, greasy sausage, soft egg and crisp chips, all washed down with a cup of hot, strong sweet tea. We couldn't linger over a second cup as it was a case of finish and make room for others. We would stroll out into the dark night and if there was time, either go for a drink or to a dance before making our way for the mass of buses to return to EK. I have since been back to Boston and wonder now how all those buses and people managed to squeeze into such a small area.

We would sing our hearts out as the bus made its way through the flat countryside, enjoying the friendships which were forged between us. We were never short of a friend, male or female, to go somewhere, to the pictures, dancing drinking etc. There was an unwritten law that there was to be "no fraternising between officers and other ranks." Well, of course they could try to keep us apart, but it was not possible.

Scotty and I would walk along the lanes towards the WAAF gates along with other couples and stop for a goodnight embrace, the warmth of our breath mingling with the cold night air and then – with flashing torches in our faces, the duty NCO would shout "Break it up everyone…" or "Come along girls, in you go…"

Further down the lane there might be a scuffle as a Waaf was saying, "I've got to go…" and in reply a pleading voice "Aw, don't go in, I may be on ops tomorrow and may not come back." It was hard to resist such a plea, which would, in all probability be true. She was torn between observing the rules or staying with her boyfriend and breaking them.

Recently, when visiting friends who are the same age as myself, I mentioned that when the "hard word" was put on me I would say, "Go and get yourself a girl from the village!" At this my friends were shocked and said in unison, "But we *were* girls from the village!"

As this was farming land, there were many haystacks dotted around, which offered comfortable and convenient facilities for 'snogging'. There was no need to ask someone where they had been when they crept into the hut late at night with bits of hay still clinging to their hair and uniform. The haystacks were also favourite hunting grounds for the duty NCOs, who would go around them in turn, flashing their torches and calling, "Lights out in

10 minutes girls, get back, break it up." There would be a lot of whispering and giggling as belts, buttons etc were hastily got together and hurried dates were made.

My 20th birthday was coming up soon and Scotty and others invited me to the pub for a celebration. We followed the line of tiny lights set in the edge of the peri track and made for the pub. The evening was magic, made even more so when Scotty said, "Here's a wee present for you Smithy…" while holding out a small package in his hand. I opened it with trembling hands, and there, sitting on a bed of velvet, was a slender gold chain with a gold cross. It was beautiful. I placed it round my neck but, of course, there was no "lily-white neck with marble-like shoulders showing above a silken gown" as there always is in Barbara Cartland's books. Instead I gently slipped the chain under my crisp, starched collar, happy in the knowledge that nestling there was such a wonderful gift. Scotty was not a man of many words, but this gave me the hope that he may feel about me as I did about him.

In the pub that evening there was a wonderful feeling of *bonhomie*. Drinks were flowing, we ordered something to eat with the drinks and some of us were able to get near to the crowded open fire. The piano player, a permanent fixture, played our favourite songs, *Don't Fence Me In*, *The Stars at Night are Big and Bright* and many of Glen Miller's tunes. My 20th birthday was celebrated well and I didn't feel at all the fact that I was not at home among my family. These men and women had become my family.

At last it was time to leave but as we walked arm-in-arm out of the warm pub, the tingling cold air took me by surprise. I had evidently enjoyed a few more shandies than I should have, and as bent down to pick up my bike I continued towards the ground, my nose hitting the gravel with a grinding sound in my ears.

"Quick!" I yelled. "Bring me a mirror." Someone produced a small torch and I held a pocket mirror to my face which revealed a red graze on the bridge of my nose - my first war wound! Getting to my feet I straddled the bike (like getting back on a horse when you're thrown) and we sang as we made our way back to camp, where I was taken to the Sergeant's mess and into a little ante-room which was already occupied with people. A jar of Vaseline was found and my nose duly "fixed". The scar from that fall has stayed with me all my life as a reminder of my 20th birthday party.

The following morning, walking down to the picket post I saluted a passing officer and she stopped me and said, "What have you done to your nose Smith?"

Of course I couldn't tell her what had actually happened, so I said, "Well Ma'am... I was cycling along on early duty call and I hit a stone with my front wheel and fell onto the gravel."

She gave me a concerned look and said, "Very well Smith, make sure you see the MO," and with that I saluted her and carried on.

Saluting officers could be a bit of a bind, especially if you were approached by an officer with whom you had been on a date the previous night. You were obliged to "fling one up", noting, as you did, the gleam in his eye.

Operations continued. Some of my friends were employed on parachute packing and if I was going in the direction of the hangar where they worked, I would look in on them. Great polished tables stretched the length of the shed where girls were busily folding parachutes meticulously into the correct order and manner, knowing only too well that any carelessness in this job would cause an airman to lose his life if his chute didn't open. The fine gossamer silk and the ropes were folded in such a way that one pull and the beautiful canopy would unfurl and gently drop the airman to safety, and hopefully on *terra firma* rather than into the sea.

Parachute silk was much coveted. My mother was fortunate in securing some and I was able to make some underwear and a blouse. I made a brassiere and French knickers, trimmed with lace, the brassiere so scanty that it did nothing at all to hold up my 34-inch bust, but it made me feel good wearing these diaphanous garments underneath my thick Air Force issue. The blouse I made had long sleeves with a jabot at the neck. I felt like a million dollars wearing those parachute clothes!

Among my friends on the station were girls who worked in the armoury. Their job was to load the ammunition belts for the air gunners. These girls worked long hours and often at unusual times when ops were 'on'. Jobs varied in the WAAF, but each helped in the war effort, no matter what it was.

The East Kirkby aircrews were now doing far more sorties than normal and when they were standing idly with a drink in their hands, chatting and laughing, a slight shaking of the hands could be observed. They were clearly working to full capacity, and perhaps beyond...

Today when films of the 1940s are shown depicting the wartime RAF it never ceases to amaze me how film directors insisted on casting 40 and 50 year olds as aircrew when, in fact, they were nearly all in the early twenties.

As the winter got colder the crews dressed in thick creamy socks worn with their flying boots, and thick woollen sweaters under their battledress tops. Of course when they were not flying they would make merry in the Mess or pubs and that helped to relieve the tension.

For some time I had noticed that I was getting more than my fair share of punishment for minor misdemeanours, such things as having hair on my collar (being curly it was a bit wayward) or wearing my stockings inside out (the thick Lyle stockings looked much better that way) and then one day, whilst giving a message to a WAAF officer, she said "Ah... so *you're* Smith," and looked at me long and hard. I mentioned this to a friend who guessed that the WAAF officers had probably heard that I had been asked out by an RAF officer and were not at all pleased I was 'poaching' on their territory.

But 'all's fair in love and war'...

On the whole, during my time in the WAAF, I found the female officers to be great. One in particular, a Signals Officer, was what I would call, "Hockey Stick", a private school zany woman. She was fun and I'm sure she had no trouble at all in keeping her RAF Officers, in fact on one occasion I arrived at the Signals Office to find the floor, my desk and typewriter, covered in a thick film of gold dust. There had been a celebration that night and a Very flame had been opened and scattered over the area.

"Sorry Smith," the WAAF Officer said, "Would you mind awfully clearing this up?" What else could I say but "Yes, Ma'am," adding "but would you please remove these…" (and they were not balloons). With a grin she returned my salute.

This was not the only floor I had cleaned. On one occasion I received jankers for some small misdemeanour and was detailed with some other Waafs to go to the Sergeants Mess and clean the floor. I didn't mind the work but what I did mind was the remarks made by the sergeants as they stood round the bar watching us … but a detail was a detail.

On the whole I wasn't caught very often!

I was due some leave and after picking up a travel warrant caught the shuttle bus for the railway station. As we stood waiting for our transport, small kit bag, gas mask and helmet at the ready, we exchanged words with some of the aircrew who were waiting for transport to take them to their dispersal points – Ops were on today.

Aircrew were always given a special breakfast, probably eggs and sausages and they carried a flask of hot tea or coffee to drink during the cold journey to the target. These flasks were very much coveted by us Waafs, and if we could scrounge them from either one of the crew or the cook house we could be assured of a hot cup of liquid for later in the evening. These flasks, along with any other non-kit articles, had to be hidden during kit inspections, though we were lucky in getting a warning when an inspection was due.

On a cold, bleak morning in flat Lincolnshire, crawling out of bed to brave the winter elements to reach the mess for breakfast before the man in white overalls joined the queue signifying "no more breakfasts would be served". As I prepared to go for breakfast there would be a call from underneath the sheets. "Hey Smithy, going to breakfast? Get me a cuppa" or "bring me some toast please Smithy" and "here's my flask, will you fill it for me Smithy". Grumbling to myself I stumbled out of the ablutions, washed, brushed my teeth, combed my hair and back to by the bed, pulled on socks, underwear, battledress, long-sleeved pullover too if it was cold. If it was very cold I would don my stiff, unbending greatcoat.

Collecting various receptacles from the lazy girls I would hop on my trusty bike and cycle down the country lane toward the mess, slithering along the icy or muddy ruts, lighting my way with an air-sea-rescue torch which I had somehow 'come by" – a length of flex with a torch battery one end and a light on the other. I would hang it round my neck like a long scarf and it would swing either side of me. With the aid of this light I could just about discern where to guide my bike.

On that particular morning, leaving the cookhouse with my battledress top bulging with toast and a couple of flasks full of tea under my arm, knife fork and spoon in my top pocket my left hand holding the handlebars I cycled past some waiting aircrew. A wolf whistle caused me to turn and in doing so I slewed the bike, sending it spinning and leaving me sprawled on the icy road, still clutching the precious flasks of tea. The cheer which went up from the crew only served to make me more angry as I gathered myself up and climbed back on my bike. Brushing the snow off my slacks with embarrassment I vowed that the girls in my hut would, in future, get their own tea!

Tea seemed to play a particularly important part of our lives. There were no special rations for the office and no special china and so, over the weeks I managed to 'procure' a selection of mugs, painting an 'S' for Signals section on the side. I also managed to scrounge tea, sugar and milk from the cookhouse and these were stowed away in the little room off the main office.

Tea time was a magnet for all types, in particular two Naval Officers attached to our base. These officers were engaged in planning "gardening" – the name given for mine-laying. Somehow they had an uncanny knack of knowing just when tea was being poured as if they had an inbuilt radar system. "Ah, Smithy is that tea we can smell…" As if they didn't know!

There was a big 'flap' on at Base and a dozen or so high-ranking officers, weighed down with "scrambled egg" (gold braid) on their caps and uniforms assembled for a meeting in a room near our Signals Office. Of course we were all agog to know what was going on and after an hour or so the door opened.

"Smith, tea for ten please," and she disappeared back into the room.

'Tea for ten!?' I was not a magician. I could not, out of the air, pluck fine china, silver and tableware. I hastily looked into my cupboard and found there were only 5 mugs, no tea and no milk. Scrambling on my bike I peddled like fury to the cookhouse, explained my errand

and with much wheedling procured extra cups, sugar, tea and milk. Back at the office I found some blotting paper and fashioned some place mats. Taking a makeshift tray along the corridor to the meeting room, I knocked, and as I was ushered in all talk stopped. There was a dead silence as I nervously placed the tray on the desk for the WAAF officer to play "mother" and then I practically genuflected out of the door. I think I would have done Lyons Corner House proud, all I needed was black stockings, high heels, short skirt, white pinny and cap – a look, it has to be said, far removed from my WAAF uniform.

Of course I was affronted at being asked to produce tea like that and if on Civvy Street I would probably have told them where to go, but … orders were orders.

Still on the subject of tea, as one of the few day-shift girls – the others were on varying shifts – I would often be called upon to do all sorts of jobs.

I recall there was a very surly Sqadron Leader. At one time he approached me and asked if I could do shorthand. I didn't like him and so said, "Sorry, Sir, I've really lost my shorthand, haven't done it for so long." He was peeved and so on one occasion, when I took him a cup of tea he shouted, "What's this Smith? What's this collar?" I looked blank. What collar? He was glaring at his cup. "There's a white collar… can't you fill the bloody cup?"

By now I had been on this station for several weeks and was due for some leave. After packing my case and collecting my travel warrant I made my way to the bus stop to take me to Stickney Railway station. As usual the train was packed and there was nothing for it but to sit on my case, filing my nails, reading and chatting with my fellow travellers. We were due for a ten minute stop at one of the stations and before the train even came to a standstill the doors of carriages were flung open and a mad dash was made for the railway café in the hope of getting a cup of tea and a bun. Of course, there was a shortage of cups, so the lucky ones who had thought to bring their own mugs were able to join the queue to be served while the rest of us went on a foraging expedition to find cups or any other sort of receptacles, flower vases, anything that could be used. There was the usual cry from the people behind the serving counter when a moan went up about the shortage of cups. "Don't you know there's a war on!" A good excuse to keep profits which were made during the war.

Back in the corridor after the stop I found myself sitting next to an airman I had seen on the station. He told me he was a runner, one of those men, it seemed, who did a mixture of all sorts of duties. His accent was an educated one and I wondered how he had been placed in the runner category – he may even have asked for that position. He was attractive, with dark complexion, brown wavy hair, longer than is usually allowed in the services and brown eyes. We chatted on all sorts of subjects during the journey and it helped to while away the hours to London.

In London the platforms were seething with people, all of whom appeared to be in a hurry, a purposeful look in their eyes. As I was not expecting anyone to meet me I made my way to the underground, the Northern Line and on to my home town of Finchley.

Once home I unpacked my things. My room was what was called 'the box room' in the house. I had four brothers and they shared, but I had a room to myself. I loved this room and guarded it jealously with instructions to Mum that my brothers were not to go into my room. But of course they did and I could tell at once if they had been in my secret hiding places. One of my aunts had given me a beautiful piece of furniture, a dressing table with many drawers, even a little secret drawer and in this I stowed, like a bower bird, all sorts of precious things. The curtains were dark maroon with field birds such as grouse and pheasants and I loved to wake up in the mornings in my sanctuary to see the morning light coming through these curtains. In the Nissen huts we had very little of the homely touches and so it was nice on leave to enjoy the simple things which made a home.

Of course during my first day on leave I contacted my special friends, none of whom had joined the services because they were working in jobs considered to be of national importance and therefore were not eligible for call up. We went up to London and joined a queue at one of the popular dance places. The queue was long and consisted of mostly servicemen and women from all parts of the world. We had a great evening and plenty of partners as we waltzed, rumba'd and quick-stepped.

On that leave I made arrangements to meet another WAAF who lived in Bayswater with her sisters and we spent some time at the Stage Door Canteen, joining a cluster of people around a small group of musicians. The pianist's fingers flashed over the keyboard, playing jazz accompanied by a guitarist, drummer and saxophonist.

The atmosphere was exciting, another world and we were part of it.

We joined the throngs of Piccadilly Circus but the lights were missing so the Old London was not there but despite the heavy bombing its major buildings appeared to be still intact. It was the Londoners themselves who had lost their homes, some of them more than once.

All too soon my leave was nearing its end. I had enjoyed staying in bed till late in the morning with Mum making a fuss of me and bringing me tea in bed.

Before joining the WAAF I did have boyfriends, one had even proposed to me at the time. I really wasn't ready for marriage and obviously I did not return his love. My mother made up my mind by saying, "It's your life; its your decision." If she had said, "No, don't marry him," who knows, out of sheer cussedness I may have made a very poor decision. I kept in touch with these boys, and from some received letters in which they declared their love, but after a while I did not reply and so while on leave I had no male contacts but instead enjoyed the dances with my girl friends.

On my return to East Kirkby, I reported to the picket post. There had been a decision that for an extra day's travelling time from leave, a day's work (jankers) was given out on the camp. It could be digging the garden beds or cleaning baths (I did do that on one occasion and spent more time outside being sick from the dirty job than inside) or it could be working in the cookhouse.

On this occasion it was to be the cookhouse, washing up. What a job! It really took the gilt off the gingerbread. During the day I broke a couple of plates and some cups and was told I would have to pay for them out of my pay. There wouldn't be much left after the breakages were paid for. But our needs were few really, and so we were able to buy a bit of make up, shampoos and other things for our personal use. Then there would be the cups of tea and coffee from the Naafi or Toc-H, a meal out of the camp, going "Dutch" when invited out by an airman and of course if stationed near home, fares for week end passes.

Sergeants Mess was having a special night and some of us were invited to join the party. Nobby Clark was a Warrant Officer and he was full of fun. I don't know what age he was, older than us I know. He was to be in charge of initiating some of us into the SSS – the Sanctimonious Scroungers Society. The bar was packed with ground staff and aircrew, standing with drinks in their hands, relaxed and ready for the fun and games.

Shaggy Dog stories were already in full spate. There was the one about a young princess locked up in the castle tower and told to stay there until a suitable husband could be found. This husband need not be of royal blood, need not be wealthy but there was one specified object the hopeful prince must get to show his prowess to the King. The princess watched as the princes bowed to the King holding a golden casket in their hands until finally, one blond-haired, blue-eyed prince was told he could have the princess for his wife, he had been successful.

The prince climbed up to the Tower window still holding the casket in his hand and when he reached the window, the princess leaning out so far that her long plaited hair tumbled toward him exclaimed, "What's this ere?" and he, the prince replied, "How did you know?" and "How did you know it was this ear," and saying this he opened the casket and there, on a cushion of purple velvet was the right ear of his slain opponent, the prize the King requested.

"This 'ere ear gives me the right to claim you for my bride." All this went on for hours, with interruptions from time to time, crossed with someone else's story, probably "what a dog to send a knight out on" or some tall story relating to the latest combat. It was all good clean fun for the kiddies. Preparations were now being made for the initiations into the Sanctimonious Scroungers Society. On a small table was a tin kettle filled with beer. We were told to kneel and had a tea towel put around our necks. When it was my turn there was a chant of "drink Smithy, drink" and "glug, glug, glug…" from the onlookers. I hated beer unless it was laced with lemonade but I did the best I could and, gasping, won the right to become a member of the SSS.

This was just one of the many ways in which we let off steam. Another was when an unsuspecting WAAF would be lunged at by a crew member, appearing to make for the chest but in fact it was the tie he was after and this was taken between his teeth and one pull, the end of the tie was torn off. It was difficult to explain to my parents why my tie had lost its end, it was all a bit crazy to them… which of course it was.

We had Australian airmen on our station and they were often seen riding several to a bike careering round the bends of the country lanes.

In April 1945 there was a tragic incident at the station. Aircraft were being prepared for a raid on targets near the Czech border and the bombs were about to be loaded from the trolleys which carried them to the aircraft. There was a huge flash as two of the one thousand pound 'cookies' exploded. We were told to get out of the area and into the nearby woods as further explosions were on the cards. Afterwards we learned that firemen were killed, three aircraft were on fire and their bombs also exploded. Some incendiaries became alight in their storage boxes. During all this a Flight Lieutenant was thrown back as he made a mad dash along the boxes to try and put out the flames, but the blast prevented this.

Medical and ambulance teams came from Conningsby and Spilsby to help with casualties, there were fourteen or more, including some civilians who were seriously hurt. They towed the bombers away to try and save them as a fourth one went up in flames and then the entire aerodrome was evacuated.

All this time we waited in the woods, not knowing the full extent of the damage but expecting the worst. We were told later that 500 and 1000 pound bombs had been fused by mistake with half-hour delay pistols. We also found out that bombs from previously 'scrubbed' ops (i.e. those cancelled at the last minute, requiring their bomb loads to be removed) were scattered around here and there and these also had been in danger of exploding.

Ruth, my first friend at East Kirkby. The Author (below)

During the night personnel from East Kirkby and the local villages heard ammunition going off and eventually all was quiet. In the morning the sight which was to meet our eyes was one of a battlefield. Six aircraft had been destroyed and fourteen others had various degrees of damage. The peritrack and runways had huge bomb craters which had to be filled in readiness for the next raid so there was a lot of work to do. We were told there was a large bomb in one of the craters which had not exploded and Bomb Disposal units were called out to trigger it off, so the hole could be filled and flattened.

630 and 57 squadron's final raids were made during that month. Victory in Europe was declared on 8th May 1945. I had been in the WAAF just over a year and felt privileged to have been part of this fantastic Bomber station.

Now the hostilities were over, it was learnt that some ground crew were going to be given a 'Cook's Tour' of Cologne and the Rhur, to see for themselves the results of the bombing campaign, but sadly there was a loss of R-Robert, one of 630's bombers and after that all Cook's Tours were cancelled. I was disappointed as I had been told that I would be on one of these trips.

Once operations were over there was a different feeling on the station; it lacked the undercurrent of excitement and tension; there was no purpose or urgency to anything anymore. As crews left for other stations and people were demobbed we partied on, fare-welling our friends who had joined up early, who were older or who had married. I was going to be demobbed when group 59's turn came, as I joined late in the war and was just 18 when I enrolled. I partied on for a further two years. The Hare &

Hounds, The Dog & Badger and The Red Lion were packed to the doorways. I farewelled Scotty, who was posted to HQ Bomber Command at High Wycombe, Buckinghamshire. I really missed him. We had worked together and spent many hours together when off duty. I mooned around for weeks but eventually had to get back into circulation. Another Signals Officer was posted to EK in Scotty's place, a very pleasant man, but the work had become humdrum.

During this period, Hilda, a girl in my hut, a pretty kitten-faced girl, asked me to accompany her to Lincoln on her next day off as she was to become engaged to her Pilot, Tim, and wanted to try on rings in the jewellers and get the correct size. I was at a loose end and so agreed we would head for Lincoln. We looked in the windows of the little shops in the steep alleyways, drooled over the clothes hanging in exclusive shop windows and had tea at 'Ye Olde Tea Shoppe', enjoying the fine china and pure white tablecloth – a change from bare wooden tables and almost unbreakable crockery.

After paying for our tea we walked out into the sunlit streets. I noticed people giving us sidelong glances and to my embarrassment I found that I was still clutching my plate, knife and fork. I had been so used to leaving the table and stacking the dishes in the cookhouse, then rinsing the "irons" (cutlery) in steaming hot water outside the mess, that it had become a habit. We rushed back to the tea shop and explained to the bewildered woman what had happened.

Time to return to East Kirkby after a wonderful day. We boarded the train and as usual it was crowded. We shared the carriage with some soldiers and they spent the time baiting and teasing us. "Look at your hands, don't look as if they've done a day's work…" and so on. We were indignant and tried to give as good as we got before lapsing into silence, we were tired as we had walked the little winding hilly streets and round the beautiful Lincoln Cathedral and were quite happy to sit and relax.

Hilda had been to the jewellers and tried on the special ring-sizer so that Tim could get her an engagement ring and so, with our mission accomplished, we were anxious now to get back to camp.

We arrived at the station and enquired about the bus to take us to camp but were told the last one had left. We had not made any enquiries as to the times of the buses and so found ourselves in a predicament. The soldiers had started to walk to their barracks and noticed we were still standing there. They came over to us and, learning that we had no way of getting back to EK, suggested we go back to their barracks with them. We drew back, unwilling to have anything to do with these soldiers who had been so rude to us previously, but after consideration we accepted their help.

Arriving at the gates to the barracks it was explained to the guard on duty what had happened and they in turn phoned the picket post. We were then taken to the post and it was arranged that Hilda and I could sleep in the NAAFI and that a guard would be posted during the night. The sergeant had eyed us up and down with a suspicious look and then convinced himself that these two young Waafs really needed his protection. Turning to the soldier he said, "Take these girls to the NAAFI and see that they are not disturbed."

This was better than nothing and once inside the empty NAAFI with a guard outside, we looked around at our surroundings. Usually the NAAFI was crowded, filled with people talking and with music, but now it was deathly quiet, the chairs stacked round the tables, the counter closed with an unfriendly finality.

Fortunately, we had eaten well in Lincoln and all that was left to do now was to try and get some sleep on the hard chairs. There were some semi-armchairs made of wicker and we settled into these, feeling uncomfortable in our uniforms. During the night I had a 'call of nature' but there was no toilet available within the building. I scouted around in the half dark, a light from a lamp nearby on the road sending a glimmer through the windows. On the shelf I spied a flower vase, dusty and without flowers. Well… I could empty it among the bushes in the morning. Meanwhile, Hilda slept like a baby. She was taller than my 5ft 7 but I just could not get into a comfortable position as I turned and twisted. At long last, from the curtain-less windows I could discern the first streaks of morning blush across the skies and daylight was nearly upon us.

There was a loud knock on the NAAFI door.

"Girls," shouted our guard, "breakfast up at the Guard Room".

Did we hear correctly? Breakfast? He was actually inviting us for breakfast. Standing up, feeling stiff and crumpled and still wearing the clothes we were wearing the day before, after a hasty comb of the hair, smoothing down our skirts we went to the door and out into the fresh morning air. We thanked our guard who said, "All in a matter of duty girls".

We were led to the Guard Room and entering saw the room had a couple of benches, a table and adjoining room which had grills in the door and from these grills a face was grimacing at us; one of the prisoners there for some misdeed or another. He started calling obscenities until the corporal told him to "shut up or else".

We sat down to a plate of greasy eggs and bacon with a slice of fried bread. It was not exactly the Ritz, but did that breakfast taste good! This was followed by a mug of hot strong sweet tea in a filthy cup, which was ignored by us and we were so grateful to the soldier who had provided this breakfast. As we ate we explained to the corporal how we happened to be in the predicament we were in and thanked him for his help and kindness. Making our way out of the Guard Room and then onto the road we asked directions to East Kirby and how far it was before starting off on our journey.

Coming into the gate was the local milkman with his daily delivery.

"Ay, Ay, Ay, what have we here, you naughty girls!" He leered at us and winked. It was no good telling him we had been guarded all night, he'd never believe us and besides, it was none of his business.

We felt refreshed with the breakfast and our spirits were high as we walked along the lanes and roads of Lincolnshire. Our hopes of getting a lift by car were dashed, there were very few private cars on the roads during the war, they were up on blocks for the duration if not in use and this being a weekend, buses were few and far between if there were any running at all.

We trudged on, stopping for a cup of tea and a biscuit at a small café. It was late when we arrived at camp, we'd been walking from breakfast time only to find our worried hut friends wondering where we had been as they had made excuses for us. They had made our beds look as though we were in them, hoping the duty corporal wouldn't look too closely.

Word got around that there was to be a big hut inspection which included a kit inspection. Our bed spaces were our own responsibility, just a small space between two beds. But it still became a chore, something which interfered with all the other important things we wanted to do. Using big tins of Mansion Polish we plopped dollops of it onto the floor and with the aid of a sanitary towel we polished the lino until it shone.

Kit was laid out in accordance, I expect, with Kings Regulations. There was a hasty hiding of articles which were not issued and which could be confiscated, such as thermos flasks, my torch etc. If any of us had a shortage of kit, we did our best to help out by passing along the missing piece of uniform or kit as the officer moved along, slowly checking.

We gave our shoes extra spit and polish … and I do mean spit. My Dad had served in the First World War and I had seen him spit on his brogues and then buff them up to a high gloss. The Duraglit was given a bashing as we polished our buttons, buckles and cap badges. I did not mind brass polishing. As a youngster at home, I had earned pocket money by polishing my brother Den's bugle when he was in the Territorials. I also polished the letterbox, house number and stair rods. What I did mind and still do mind is window cleaning. Each day two WAAF were detailed for hut duty and they had to clean the centre of the hut, make sure the windows were clean and do some of the jobs which were not included in the individual bed spaces. I recall one girl in particular in our hut had a job to hide her non-kit items. Her duties had been to go through the personal effects of men who had not come back from a raid. All valuable items were carefully catalogued and the men's cars were kept in a compound awaiting instructions from their next of kin, but sweets, for instance, could not be itemized. I'm sure she felt great sadness while doing her job and had to become hardened to it but we, in the hut, could not bring ourselves to accept the offer of one of those sweets.

Sweets we did enjoy were the Horlicks tablets which we scrounged from equipment used in the Air/Sea Rescue boats. We would munch the forbidden fruits with relish, convinced they were doing us good. Our huts were made as liveable as possible. On the shelves above the beds would be family photographs and photos of boyfriends.

One girl in our hut appeared to be what was then called a jinx. On more than one occasion she became engaged to a crew member and the engagement ended sadly when her fiancé was killed on a raid. On her bed-side she had a few large studio photos of these men and I would see the dim red glow of a cigarette as she smoked into the early hours of the morning trying to come to grips with the tragedies of war.

If one thought with one's head about love, ground crew would have been chosen as opposed to the aircrew, but of course that is not the way it worked...

Another girl in the hut was baby crazy and had her wall covered with pictures cut out from magazines of babies in all shapes and sizes. I, on the other hand, had pictures of my favourite film stars. There was one of Lena Horne, her dark skin enhanced by a long white silky gown; there was Rita Hayworth, long thick wavy hair tumbling around her shoulders and Gary Cooper – Coop – with his broad, shy smile looking out at me from the wall. Pictures of boyfriends, I kept close to my heart in my wallet.

If one of the hut members was going on a weekend pass with a friend, all drawers were searched for our best finery and we would send her on her way with a bit of silky glamour.

We did get on very well, considering there were women from all walks of life living and sharing a fairly small area. We often played jokes on someone, especially if we knew she could take a joke. On one occasion whilst the girl was out on a date we removed her bed into a nearby field, covered it with a groundsheet to keep it from the damp night air, pushed all the beds up to close the gap and waited...

Of course we all thought it a huge joke when she thought she had made a mistake and come into the wrong hut.

Also among us was a woman who could only be called a "man-eater". She was married, tall, blond and older than most of us. She was far more experienced with men than we were and the men were flattered by her attentions. She had no compunction in manoeuvring a boy-friend away from any of us.

There was a weekly dance and it was in full swing. We were standing around talking and waiting for the next dance. I was with a group of men I knew, enjoying a drink and chat when one of the crowd gave a low whis-tle. Into the hall, making a late entrance was the "man-eater". She looked stunning in a clinging jumper, straight tight skirt, silk stockings and high-heeled shoes. This woman had used the time to go through our bomb boxes (boxes under the bed for odds and ends) and our drawers to select articles she knew she would look good in.

I was piqued as my friends turned to look and made a catty remark "Oh yes, she does look great but she's quite old you know, at least 27". This didn't deter the men and as I said before they found the more mature women more attractive and of course more knowing.

We servicewomen were sometimes disadvantaged when our boyfriend also had a girl in his home town. He would see us day in and day out, with colds, in bad moods, in uniform. When he went home his girl would have spent hours manicuring her nails, shampooing her hair, pressing her pretty silky dress and be there waiting for him. We could do nothing about the situation and often were the losers. Of course there were "plenty more fish in the sea" and we were never short of a date, but often we were not always aware that our date was mar-ried, which of course caused heartache when the truth became known.

Now that ops were no longer in progress and the war in Europe was over we had more time off and would take rides around the countryside on our bikes. Three of us took to the lanes and, stopping by the side of the road under a tall brick wall, we sat resting until we spied apples hanging over the wall. These apples were my favourite: Cox's Orange Pippins.

"Put your bike against the wall, climb up and slip over into the orchard," someone suggested. One of us kept a lookout as Babs clambered up and over.

"Throw your hat over, then I can collect more," she called.

Over the top went a much-battered cap.

"Hullo there…" came a woman's voice. We hadn't seen her approaching; we'd been so intent on scrumping. She was a woman of about 50, wearing a twin-set of fine wool, a straight plaid skirt and flat walking shoes. She was short and plump, her sandy-coloured hair done up in a wispy knot at the back of her head. She was as surprised as us to hear Babs call, "I'm going to throw these over the wall then I can climb up, watch out."

By this time the woman had opened the double gates and was peering round the corner at the WAAF busily scrumping her best apples.

"Wouldn't you like to come up to the house and have some tea?" she said, smiling. "I've some freshly-picked apples you can take with you."

We felt so small and mean being caught scrumping.

We walked with her along the gravel path, leaving our bikes at the gate and approached a small stone cottage, with printed curtains blowing gently through the open windows. Entering the hall there came to us the smells of furniture and floor polish, baking and freshly picked flowers. It was a "lived-in" house.

"My son is in the Navy," she said, pointing to a framed photograph on top of the piano, showing a smiling Petty Officer. "I do miss him and I hope you will all call again and see me. I really would like that." As she spoke she busied herself pouring tea and cutting thick slices of home-made cake. We forgot that we had been caught in her grounds stealing her apples as we sat in the deep-cushioned, chinz-covered chairs. We were enjoying the mothering and were loathe to say goodbye. We left carrying a brown paper bag full of Cox's Orange Pippins promising, as we turned to wave to her as she stood at the door, that we would love to see her again.

Further along the road from the camp was Revesby Manor and one of the Manor's neighbours was a lady who advertised on a board outside her garden, "Honey for Sale". We would walk along to this cottage and purchase a jar of her honey to take home to our family, a very welcome addition to a sparse sugar ration. On our first visit she kindly demonstrated her technique of spinning the honeycomb to release the golden nectar. Many years later I was to learn that that same lady was still selling her honey.

Often we would cycle further afield than our camp at East Kirkby. Sports afternoon would see an exodus from the camp of all ranks making our own sports arrangements. We would set off along the straight roads, the stiff cold winds making it necessary for us to bend our bodies against the driving force cycling toward Mablethorpe or Skegness, the flat fenlands either side of us. It was wonderful to cycle these roads and feel the fresh air coursing down into our lungs. We at Base HQ had no fresh air straight through the open windows. It was brought in through large square pipes and so we particularly loved to be out in the fresh air.

We would stop for lunch at a café then ride on towards the sea. The sands were hedged with barbed wire and tank traps to keep the enemy at bay should they attempt a landing. We would manage to scout round these obstacles and sit on our jackets or rain capes listening to the sounds of the lapping waves and the screeching of the gulls as they swooped and dived for their meal. It was difficult to tear ourselves away from the sparkling waters to make our way back to camp.

The war in Europe was over and aircrew and other personnel were being posted to different stations while others were demobbed, returning to civvy street.

As for me, I was enjoying myself, although along with everyone else we still came out with "I'm browned off" or "I'm cheesed off" as the work now appeared boring. One particular job was in that category – it was keeping the book of Kings Regulations up to date which entailed cutting slithers of notes out of a page and sticking into another – browned off, yes.

Of course with no more operations we had no trouble in keeping dates for dances, pictures or a drink at the local pub. Previously, there was no certainty that your date would be able to join you at the time arranged.

During August of 1945 a posting came through for me to Chicksands Priory Signals Station. I had mixed feelings as I had been saying goodbye to a great many friends and associates I had known during the past 12 months and now I would be off to fresh fields and new faces. Of course there had to be a farewell party, but this time I made quite sure I stayed on my bike when leaving Red Lion!

It was a feeling of great regret that I left this operational station which had made history. Years later a Memorial was built to those who lost their lives flying with 57 and 630 Squadrons. The runways would return to the farmers but the Control Tower, after years of neglect, was lovingly rebuilt and became part of the Aviation Heritage Centre.

A poem was sent to me by a WAAF friend which, as I read it, brought tears to my eyes and such a feeling of sadness and loss. It was called "Old Airfield" and was written by W. Scott, ex-630 squadron.

OLD AIRFIELD

I lie beside the hill
Abandoned long to Nature's will
My buildings down, my people gone
My only sounds the wild birdsong.

My mighty birds will rise no more
No more I hear the Merlins roar
And never now my bosom feels
The pounding of their giant wheels

From ancient hills their voices blast
Thunderous echoes of the past
And still in lonely reverie
Their great dark wings sweep down to me.

Laughter, sorrow, hope and pain
I shall never know these things again
Emotions that I came to know
Of strange young men so long ago.

Who knows as evening shadows meet
Are they with me still, a phantom fleet?
And do my ghosts still stride unseen
Across my face so wide and green?

In future should some structure tall,
Bury me beyond recall,
I shall still remember them,
My metal birds and long dead men.

Now weeds grow high, obscure the sky
Remember me when you pass by,
Beneath this tangled, leafy screen
I was your home, your friend "Silksheen".

The former control tower and War Memorial at RAF East Kirkby

Lancaster on display at East Kirkby Aviation Centre, Lincoln.

Outside our hut at East Kirkby.
(l to r) Joan Couzens, Dot Brailsford, Marie Lord, Eileen Smith.

'Sports Afternoon' on the sands.
The Author with tank traps in background.

Some of the staff of the Signals Section, RAF East Kirkby 1945.

Some of the staff of the Signals Section, RAF East Kirkby 1945.

Sergeants Mess, RAF East Kirkby. Nobby Clark i/c Sanctimonious Scroungers Society.

RAF East Kirkby march-past; a farewell to an Australian squadron.

6. Chicksands Priory

I arrived at Chicksands and made myself known at the picket post, where I was given the usual 'arrival chit' to be filled in, plus all the usual bed sheets, pillow case etc and was told which hut number to go to. I found the hut but it was empty of people. There was one bed, which appeared to be mine, three biscuits and a bare wire base. I made up the bed, put my feather cushion, which travelled everywhere with me, in place of the bullet-like bolster pillow and prepared for an early night.

I had been travelling most of the day; the trains had been slow with many stoppages and delays. I was just dozing off when I heard a loud cockney voice shouting "Who the blinking hell is this?" and "Who she fink she is, dossing down and letting the stove go out!"

I lay there in my cold bed, eyes still closed, realizing that the person talking in those dulcet tones was referring to me. I sat up and, whereas a few months ago I would have been a shrinking violet, made it quite clear that this was the hut I had been allocated by the picket post.

Fortunately for me, the rest of the girls were friendlier and invited me to the NAAFI for a cup of coffee or tea. I gladly accepted the invitation and put my battledress over my striped blue and white pyjamas.

Chicksands Priory was set among beautiful woodlands and I realized soon that it could be quite nice here. The following day, presenting myself to the Orderly Room, I was told that there was no similar job to that which I had been doing at East Kirkby and so I was to learn the ropes of the Camp Post Office.

The corporal in charge of the Post Office was Elsie Ashford, a quietly-spoken girl from Southampton with a slight Hampshire burr in her voice. She was very pleasant and patient and made me feel very welcome.

There were two other people in the office. One was Tubby, a Cornishman with dark brown wavy hair, rosy cheeks and a bit on the plump side. He was ex-aircrew, as was the other man, Dixie. We four ran the Post Office, not only efficiently, but with great fun, which made the job more enjoyable. Tubby had a great fund of sayings and jokes and would keep us entertained as we sorted the mail into pigeon holes when it came in from Shefford in big sacks. On the backs of some envelopes would be 'SWALK' (Sealed With A Loving Kiss) or big lipstick lips for some lucky person. We only hoped there would be some for us too.

At certain times of the day we would go round the station collecting mail to be posted. Officers were housed in the old Priory and Tex, a tall Jamaican airman who drove the van, singing in a beautiful voice, would wait outside the Priory while I made the collection from a table in the hall.

The Priory was said to have a resident ghost. Many years ago, in the previous century, a nun called Rosanna had fallen madly in love with a monk from a nearby monastery. When the affair was discovered she was walled up alive in the Priory and there was said to be a plaque in the hall telling of this. I always felt ill-at-ease entering the hall to deliver and collect the mail, especially on the day she was said to walk.

After bagging the mail we made for the Shefford Post Office, picking up any mail for the camp and signing the registry. It was a fun job; I loved it, especially as it meant freedom from being captive at a desk.

Tubby asked me out on a date and I accepted, despite reports from other girls who had already been out with him – "He ripped my bra", "He went wild" or "He tore my skirt. I waited for the moment when I would have to fight tooth and nail for my honour but I needn't have worried, there was nothing to report to the girls back in the hut, Tubby behaved like a perfect gentleman and as usual had been good company. The stories must have been made up to make the other girls' dates sound more exciting – unless of course it was a case of "you get what you ask for". My mother spoilt my WAAF days, I jokingly said, because she told a friend "I know I can trust Eileen!"

At Chicksands the Orderly Room was run by a very efficient but stern Flight Sergeant. He was a straight-backed regular; no nonsense and no fun. He certainly was not at all happy that I was enjoying myself in my job at the Camp Post Office. After a couple of months there was a vacancy in his office and I was told I would be more useful in the Orderly Room. As I presented myself for the job he pointed to a desk opposite him.

"You'll sit there Smith, where I can keep an eye on you". I was annoyed by his attitude, at this point I don't think there was a single entry on my charge sheet.

My duties were what was known as 'P2 Clerk Officers Personal Occurrence Reports'. All personal movements such as leave, sick leave, promotions, marriages, etc had to be recorded.

The job had one advantage, though. We Waafs were not always aware whether our dates were married or not and very rarely did they tell us, but in the case of the officers, I now had access to all that information, though of course it was strictly for my eyes and information only!

In the course of the day, my desk would become covered in all sorts of odd bits of paper containing the latest pieces of information to be added to the records. It was a messy job but not unbearable.

There were many former aircrew who, like myself, had been posted from previously operational Bomber Command stations. I noted that 'Flight' appeared to give these men rather menial duties, not befitting their status. Maybe he felt hard-done-by in that he had not been involved in any flying and therefore felt bitter towards them. I foiled him on some occasions and I took some menial duties from them, like sweeping the floor, fetching tea, etc.

One of the chaps in the OR was Mark, who was tall with fair, wavy hair and very good looking. His uniform was immaculate, his shoulders padded out, looking like "Garth" of the comic strip, the creases of his battledress razor sharp, his whistle at a jaunty angle. Mark was a very pleasant type and he, in particular, appreciated my efforts to save him the indignity of doing menial jobs.

We both lived near London and would often travel together on our long weekends off, hitching rides if possible. Mark a snob, especially a car snob, he wouldn't accept a lift from just any old car and would grandly wave on the kind driver sitting at the wheel of a less than new car. Mark would only accept a lift for us, even for a shorter trip than we wanted, in a Bentley, a Wolsley or someother type of classic sports car, sitting back among the leather upholstered seats, wearing a smug, spoilt look.

On VE Day some of us were not so choosy as to the mode of transport as we thumbed our way to London. We arrived near the centre of the city on the back of a lorry, perched on top of a stack of gas cylinders, hanging on grimly as we rounded corners and eventually dropping down onto the pavement, ready to join in the celebrations.

We moved along with the crowds to Buckingham Palace and joined in the chanting for the King and Queen to come out on to the balcony, afterwards milling around town laughing and happy that at least the war in Europe was over. No more bombing, no more sleepless nights, no more separation from the families and friends. Of course, I was not to know that I would not be demobbed until August 1947. By then, most of the world had settled down to normality, but really I was in no hurry to get out. Of course some of those serving had been in uniform from the word go in September 1939 when I was still in drill slips and navy blue knickers, like one of Ronald Serle's little girls (only not so little).

Back at Chicksands Priory, work continued like any well organized firm; everyone knew their duties and we just got on with them. During off-duty times we found plenty to do; plenty of amusements. Often we would go in a group to Bedford, the nearest big town. We would pair off, rent out rowing boats and row along the River Ouse in leisurely fashion – that is, until an oar went overboard, then it was all hands to retrieve it, everyone grappling over the sides of the boats in their excitement and nearly falling overboard themselves.

The Corn Exchange in Bedford held dances and quite a few of Britain's top Big Bands played there. We were fortunate enough to be there when Glen Miller's band played and we quickstepped to the distinctive sound of *String of Pearls*, *Moonlight Serenade* and *In the Mood* – and we certainly *were* in the mood – jiving and dancing to near exhaustion. After the dance, on the way back to camp in the bus we sang some of the favourite songs of the day, such as Frank Sinatra's *Nancy with the Laughing Eyes* or *Don't Fence Me In* and *Don't Get Around Much Any More*, carrying on down the lane until we reached our compounds. If, on the other hand, we were with a boyfriend, we would linger among the sweet-smelling bushes until it was time to go in.

Sandy Lane could be a frightening place and on one occasion I had gone home by bus, the journey to Finchley being about 27 miles. We were having a special dance on the station and we could wear civilian clothes. I took the bus back to Chicksands, arriving mid-evening. I had been happy sitting in the bus in the company of several airmen, but when we reached the men's camp entrance everyone got off, leaving me to go the last half mile in the bus on my own. If I had realized, I could have alighted at the other entrance and walked up to the WAAF quarters. I really don't know why I was frightened, there had been no attacks, but of course there was Rosanna the ghost and it was a very dark lane with deep forest either side. As I stepped off the bus my mouth was dry; I hastily looked right and left then, eyes firmly on the flashing red pylon, made a dash for camp.

On another occasion a similar thing happened and this time I was not aware that the bus did not go past the station but stopped at the village. Once more I was on my own. Ahead stretched the dimly-lit road which went past the RAF gates and on to Sandy Lane; on one side of the road was the cemetery and further along was a tree where it was said a hangman's noose was put in medieval days. I think I could have won an Olympic gold medal for the time I made in my race to the safety of our hut.

Our rations were substantial in the Air Force but we always seemed to be hungry and if money permitted we would hitch a ride to a café which sold egg and chips. We enjoyed the crispy golden chips and it was worth the effort to crawl past the picket post and hitch a ride. After the meal, if the money would stretch to it, we would have a drink at the local pub where we would enjoy a game of darts or, if the piano player was there, would stand around singing before making our way back to camp.

We were sometimes treated to an ENSA concert by those wonderful entertainers who gave of their time to entertain the troops. During the war, some of the troops overseas had been entertained by top-name acts, but now that hostilities were over the entertainers were of the less-than-famous variety. One act I recall was 'The Fairy'. No longer a young woman, her much-used fairy costume no longer pristine white, she would balance on tiptoe on a big coloured ball and move across the stage in what must have been a very difficult feat. We applauded her – and every other act – with gusto.

On one occasion Henlow RAF Station invited us all to attend their 'Gaiety Old Time Music Hall'. We piled out of the buses into the hall, which had been turned into a scene of the olden days. The floor was strewn with sawdust and the menu included meats, salads and sausages, sausage rolls and of course beer and minerals, the latter for 6d and "best beer" a shilling. The cast included some RAF personnel who were later to become well-known in radio, TV and films, including Alfred Marks, Eric Sykes, Frank Muir and Dennis Norden.

The Gaiety Girls were all members of Henlow WAAF Station. There was a sing-along and the programme said, "You are invited to join in the second chorus". The songs included, *Who's Your Lady Friend*, *Sister Susie* and *My Old Dutch*. By the end of the evening our throats were dry with singing and shouting.

The Programme from the show.

MUSIC HALL

Produced by :	A/C Dave Aylott
Scenery constructed under the direction of :	Cpl. Johnny Russell
Executed by :	L.A.C's. F. Chaventre, A. Sykes and A/C T. Rice
Designed by :	Jack Duke
Musical Direction and Orchestrations :	W/O W. Parsons
Script and continuity :	L.A.C. Frank Muir and A/C Dave Aylott
Business direction :	F/O Hugh Louden
Dances arranged by :	L.A.C. Alfred Marks
House manager :	A/C Ben Arbeid

CAST

Totty Gay	L.A.C.W. Gabrielle Hamilton
Betty Lily	L.A.C.W. Lily Garlick
Patty Wingco	Patsy Beadle
The Great Gus Herbert	L.A.C. Frank Muir
Slasher Albert	L.A.C. George Lower
Freddie Dander	A/C Dave Aylott
Alfredo Marks	L.A.C. Alfred Marks
Montague Button	L.A.C. W. Alden-Montague
Obadiah Long	L.A.C. Ronald Short
Tom Sweeter	L.A.C. Tom Morgan
Bertie Bernard	L.A.C. Bernard Graham
Sammy Skimpole	Cpl. Thorne

THE GAIETY GIRLS

L.A.C.W's. - Bobby Summerfield, Peggy Skeats, Sylvia Colloff, Doris Stickland, Margaret Davis, and Miss Patsy Beadle.

The cast list.

It was about this time I received my second "war wound". I had moved into Elsie's hut, where she was the corporal-in-charge. Elsie was and is the kindest person and would do anything for anybody, so when I made the remark that I didn't like going along the paths at night to the ablutions she immediately said "just give me shake and I'll come with you". I just couldn't refuse such an offer and so that evening I shook her and shook her until finally she opened her bleary eyes.

"Remember," I said, "you said you'd come with me to the ablutions." I really think at that time of night she regretted making such a rash offer, but she climbed into her plimsoles and we made our way out into the freezing cold night air and along by the huts, missing the makeshift clothes lines which straddled between the small trees and then…

"Elsie!" I yelled, as I disappeared down into the depths of a manhole. Elsie came running back, flashing her torch to see why all the fuss. I had walked on a cracked manhole cover, probably cracked when a delivery van went over it. My right led had disappeared into some pipes, my plimsole was missing and above my knee an ugly gash was oozing blood.

With difficulty I climbed out of the hole and we somehow got back to the hut. By now everyone was wide awake as we put on the light to see what damage had been done. There was no First Aid kit and no running water so a bright girl suggested we open a water bottle and clean the wound. There was not a thought in our minds that the water could do more harm than good. Following day I was up early and reported for sick parade.

We had to be pretty sick to get up so early and also be sick enough not to be reported for malingering. I really don't think the MO believed me when I recalled my midnight mishap down among the drains.

Later on in my married days living in Australia I had a similar accident. I had finished my housework, had a shower and put on a long floral dress for the evening. Something caught my eye, and, looking up at the ceiling I spied a thin line of very busy ants. I couldn't let them take over my house so I stood up on the toilet seat and took aim with a can of fly spray... Just as I was about to open fire the toilet seat gave way and my right leg – the leg I had hurt down the manhole – went right through and down to the s-bend, I fell backwards, hitting my head on the stone floor. It could have been a horrendous home accident, but apart from a big tear on my shin and bruising on both legs, that was it. We made our way to the local hospital and after a long wait, as it was by now eight o'clock in the evening, I saw the Doctor. It took great courage for me to tell him how I got my jagged cut! Here was a lady all dolled-up for the evening's fun and games in a long dress declaring that she had fallen down the toilet! Several stitches were put into the wound and along with my manhole scar and my bicycle scar it is still there to remind me of days gone by!

Our hut was quite near the cookhouse and this made it a nice warm haven for some of the creatures which scrounged food and crumbs from the dustbins and floors of the cooking area. On one occasion, tucked up in bed and sleeping soundly, lights out and the door left ajar for some of the girls who were still out on a binge and due back later.

Coming out of this deep sleep I was awakened by a loud commotion. The girls were back in the hut and entering had spied a rat in the doorway. Apparently they had grabbed the broom and chased it into a corner where it had its back to the wall, screeching, squealing and jumping up and the girls, in their turn were shrieking and laughing at the same time as they were in a very 'happy' state from their party. The rat was getting desperate and wanted his escape but an airman from the cookhouse had now grabbed the broom from the girl and as he did so it escaped the corner, finishing up under the bed beside mine. I lay petrified, watching the gruesome proceedings until, with a hefty swipe of the broom, it was killed in my bed space, leaving a distinct outline of the rat on the lino as it was carried by it's long thin tail.

It was difficult to get back to sleep again after that!

We were very well fed, three good meals a day and certainly more food than we had had with rationing during the years before we joined up. Apart from the provided meals there was the NAAFI van which travelled around the compounds at break times selling hot coffee, tea cakes for a nominal price. On hearing the hooter of the van, it was a case of first sighted first out and a mad dash clutching ones mug. The 'wads', as they were called, were layers of multi coloured sponge, kept together with mock cream and these were very much a filler for morning or afternoon tea. The Toc-H was also there for us with the insignia of a lamp depicting a light shining. It was often the remark he or she "was as dim as a Toc-H lamp." The Toc-H was installed in the village hall and that was another venue to meet, chat and have some supper.

The women serving us in the NAAFI were a wonderful crowd, they were kept busy serving us and would go out of their way to please us whilst at the same time keeping us all in our place.

Elsie and I were very partial to mushrooms and one day we decided to go foraging in the nearby fields. There among the dewy grass were small white gleaming mushrooms and we filled our hats with these jewels and made for the NAAFI.

"Audrey, do you think you could do us a favour and cook these mushrooms for us, maybe you could put them with a sausage or something please."

Audrey looked at us with raised eyebrows. "Well now madams what palates you must have." We weren't sure whether she approved of our mixture but she did fry the mushrooms for us which made a change from the usual diet we were given.

On the subject of food, if we were on duty over the weekend that is after the war had ended, one dish which has stuck in my memory is the Sunday trifle. The trifle was huge, I must think it was made according to Kings Regulations as I have spoken to many ex-service personnel and they too remember it. The top was decorated with mock cream and to us it was absolutely scrumptious.

I had now reached the dizzy heights of LACW, Leading Aircraftswoman. This gave me the right to wear a propeller badge on my sleeve. For the privilege of being an LACW came extra duties and one of these was to be on duty in the Orderly Room over the weekend. Phone messages were taken, queries answered and travel warrants issued. Now that was scary, not for me, but for the person going on leave. My sense of direction was and is terrible. Reading maps is not my forte and so I filled in the travel warrants, decided which mode of transport and which stops and ports whilst trying to avoid the trusting eyes of the WAAF or RAF going off on leave. I shall never know if anyone was Missing on Leave due to my lack of direction.

On one of these weekend duties I asked a friend if she would keep me company and she agreed but said she would be there later in the evening as she had a date. It was deathly quiet, seated at the desk reading, the phone rang, making me jump out of my skin.

"Hello, Orderly Room, WAAF Smith speaking."

"Hi there Smithy!" It was a young Education Officer who was often in a party with us. he was ringing to see how I was faring in my lonely post and to let me share in the fun and games going on in the Officers Mess.

There was a piercing shriek and I heard a woman's voice shouting and shrieking.

"What's that?" I said quaking in my lace-up issue shoes.

"Not to worry Smithy, just Section Officer being up-ended, nothing to worry about at all," and with that he said goodbye and hung up.

All became quiet again when a rustling sound from the corner of the room made my ears tingle as I strained to catch the sound. Knees knocking, I picked up a heavy pencil sharpener and crossed the room to where I thought the noise was coming from. As I reached the stove there was a flurry of soot from the fireplace and a bird emerged, covered in soot. It flew past me, wings flapping and making piercing sounds, beak wide open and I too screamed. It made for the window, battering its little body against the window in an effort to escape.

This was the very night Rosanna was said to walk the Priory grounds, the night when sights were seen all over the place and the night when I too had had a 'visitation'…

Down by the Priory was a bridge with a small brook running under it and through the camp. On such a night as this an eerie fog would curl up from the water and over the bridge, making a perfect background for the blood-curdling howls which now emitted from cloth-shrouded 'ghosts' as they glided about the station with the intention of scaring the brass buttons off our uniforms!

I had been at Chicksands Signals Station long enough to be eligible for some leave and Elsie from the Post Office had invited me down to her home in Southampton. Packing my small kit and other personal belongings, I caught the bus to London then the train to Southampton. I arrived in the early evening and joined the throng of travellers leaving the train and making their way along the platform and over the bridge. I saw what looked like a big red wall in the distance. On closer inspection I realized it was one of the funnels of a huge liner. Later when I mentioned this to Elsie I was told it was the *Queen Mary,* which had been used during the war as a troop ship. I hadn't realized what a huge ship it was.

We had a wonderful few days leave. This was the part of England I did not know, in fact, I did not, at that time,

know much about England as at the outbreak of the war I
had been only 14. My trips, apart from emigrating from
England to Canada in my early childhood, had been by
my bike from Finchley through the country roads to
London to Colney near St Albans where my favourite
Aunt Elsie lived. Then of course there had been London
to Wilmslow and the surrounding Cheshire, seen mostly
on route marches, then East Kirkby and finally Chicksands, so it was a pleasure to see another part of the
country. We visited beaches, shops and beautiful gardens
in Bournemouth. The war was over now and things
appeared to be getting back to normal. We found a small
cosy looking café in a side street and on ordering our tea
looked around us. The atmosphere was one of gentility:
quiet, subdued talking and a far off clatter of china in the
kitchen, so different from the noisy banter and clatter of
dishes in the camp mess. As we sat, enjoying the potted
palms, dainty china and pretty tablecloths there came the
sound of music drifting down from above. Looking up
we saw, among the brown velvet curtains, three little
ladies playing cello, violin and piano, a mini palm court
orchestra for the patron's pleasure, making the whole
scene just perfect.

Back at Chicksands after a wonderful few days leave,
during a tea break Mark took me aside and said, "Whilst
on leave I met someone who knows you…" Further
questioning led me to believe that the person who knew
me was Scotty. I had received no letters from him and
from this I presumed that I had seen more in our friendship than he. It had also dawned on me that he was
probably married – after all, he was about five years my

senior and in the regular Air Force. He had been yet another ship which passed in the night. I hopefully clung to the thought that at least he had remembered me enough to mention me to Mark, so I wrote to him and received a reply quite shortly after posting it.

We picked up the threads of our friendship and often met in London. We had meals at the Cumberland Hotel; food I had not tasted for years. We saw films in Leicester Square, queuing and spending time talking and finding out about each other. I was on Cloud Nine to be once more spending time with the man I had 'carried a torch for' for over a year, although I was still dating men at camp; there was no shortage of partners to go dancing with or to a film.

Many of my friends were now engaged to be married as now the war was over couples felt the time was right to marry and have children. In our Orderly Room, a pretty Waaf with blonde hair blue, kitten-like eyes was engaged to a sweet RAF chap who also worked in the Orderly Room. They were to be married at Chicksands, then off on honeymoon. We helped Jean prepared for her special day by virtually acting as bridesmaids and assisting where we could. She looked beautiful and it was wonderful to see, after all the drabness of the war, such a glittering, beautifully-gowned young woman.

Thousands were being demobbed daily from the services or being posted to other stations and our Orderly Room Flight Sergeant, still stiff-backed and miserable, couldn't wait for us all to go too, so it was with relish and a glint in his eye that he called me over to his desk and with just a little twitch of his mouth which could even have been a smile, said, "You're posted Smith".

I had expected to remain at Chicksands until my de-mob number (Group 59) came up, but as it turned out it was to be a further year before I was demobbed.

"You're posted to Medmenham, 90 Group, it's in Buckinghamshire."

I knew the area only because Scotty had been posted to HQ Bomber Command. In no time at all I had completed my 'clearance chit' and said goodbye to my friends. One girl in particular I would miss, I had met at East Kirkby, where she was known to us as Rene (pronounced 'Reeny'); she always looked as if she had slept in her clothes, which were creased and un-pressed with wrinkled none-too-clean shoes, but she was a cheerful girl and we all liked her. The next time I met her was in the NAAFI at Chicksands. A group of RAF chaps and Waafs were sitting round a table listening to classical music and there, among them, looking slim, trim and immaculate, was Rene … or so I thought.

I made myself known to her.

"I'm Renée now…" she said (pronouncing it Ren-*ay).*

She had gone all French! I could only assume her transformation had come about from her association with her boyfriend, a handsome RAF chap now by her side.

Rene/Renée was the only girl I met up with twice in the course of my WAAF service. I have no idea what happened to Squibs, Barbara and the others of my intake, where they were posted or what courses they eventually did. I hope that, like me, they enjoyed their time in the WAAF.

Cpl Elsie Ashford, on leave at Bournemouth.

On leave in London, LACW Smith and friend Betty (cheesed off with pavement photographer!).

7. Medmenham

Here I was, once more on a strange new station. Reporting to the person in charge at the picket post I was given my hut number and directions to find it.

This station was very different from my previous postings. East Kirkby was in open fields with huts and other buildings dispersed in all directions – Nissen huts, which were hot in summer and cold in winter.

Chicksands Priory was a little more condensed, with some made up paths and roads, but Medmenham was completely different. The huts were all situated off a covered hallway and this appeared to be far more sensible than having the unsheltered doors open to the elements. Apparently the US Air Force had occupied Medmenham prior to the RAF.

Medmenham was in the grounds of a beautiful country house, with manicured lawns and tall privet hedges topiaried into wonderful shapes. There were peacocks roaming among the grounds, making their own peculiar noises and further down into the gardens was a pond with water littlies and goldfish and overseeing it all, a cherub with its urn tipping water from the top of a waterfall.

Only recently that I learned that Medmenham was the place where RAF air reconnaissance photographs were analysed, with the discovery on one occasion, of the place where the V1 launch sites were hidden. But, by the time

I arrived all wartime activities were finished and left for historians to record. Once more my duties were to be P2, Officers records and POR, Personal Occurrence Reports.

My office was attached to the Commanding Officer and Station Adjutant's office. In the office were three other clerks – a WAAF and two Jamaican airmen. We worked well together and on the whole kept pretty busy. I did secretarial work for the CO and one job in particular, which somehow I was responsible for, was the Establishment Sheets. No one, and I mean no one, ever told me what or how to do it or what was its use. I floundered through the maze of postings and supernumerary happenings until one day, several weeks later, I was called to the office of the Officer who had given me the job. I entered his office, flinging one up, and he said "Smith, what on earth are you doing with these figures? I can't make sense of this."

"And Neither can I … Sir" I replied.

Fortunately for me, this piece of bad workmanship made no difference to my reaching the dizzy heights of Corporal. I was an NCO! When I was notified of my rank change the CO stopped me, smiled and said "I expect you will be off home this weekend to show off your tapes to your parents Smith."

"No, Sir," I replied, "I haven't received them yet."

I informed him that on enquiring of the WAAF Officer why my corporal status had not come through, she replied that they had not as yet recorded it.

"We'll soon see about that…" the CO said, and the very next weekend I was wearing my two stripes.

As a corporal, one duty which befell me was to accompany the Duty Officer of the Day on his mess hall inspection. She or he would walk ahead, with me in tow.

"Any complaints?" he would ask, hands behind his back, head bent enquiringly over someone's greasy plate.

I found it hard to keep a straight face, remembering an occasion when a very young officer asked me the same question.

"Yes, Sir," I replied, "I do have a complaint."

He went red, pulled out his little notebook and pencil from his top pocket and asked, "What is it them?"

"My dinner is always cold, sir," I replied.

He wrote this down and went on his way, and I hoped that I had done him a favour by giving him something to report.

That afternoon the WAAF Officer called me into her office and said, "I believe you have a complaint about your food Smith."

"Yes, Ma'am," I said, standing to attention.

"Well do you make a habit of complaining about your food Smith?"

"No Ma'am." I looked straight ahead, "but I felt sorry for him."

The WAAF Officer lifted her eyebrows to her hairline and sighed. "Very well Smith, you may go."

I saluted, about-turned and smartly stepped out of the office.

Being a corporal also meant that I was now in charge of a hut full of Waafs. I was lucky; we all got on so well together and if there was one who did not pull her weight in cleaning etc, a quiet reminder to her in private was all that was needed and all was well.

Near Medmenham was the town of Marlow and on sports afternoons some of us would go for a splash and swim in the Thames River swimming baths. I wasn't at all keen on swimming in the muddy water with reeds below my feet and squashy mud between my toes. As my brother-in-law Bob once said, "I like swimming with blue tiles under my feet".

Marlow was known for its restaurant, *The Compleat Angler*, set in lovely grounds with carpet-like lawns going down to the river's edge. On one of our meetings Scotty took me to the *Compleat Angler* and we had a wonderful meal together. I had my first ever Pimms No. 1, the delicate flavour enhanced by additional fruits placed on top.

After the meal, watching the boats on the water, I felt happy and relaxed, that is until I noticed two very glamorous women sitting at the bar on high stools, their long civilian legs covered in fine silk stockings. I intercepted a glance between one of these women and my escort Scotty. I was hurt and baffled. Had Scotty met these women before and who or what were they? I was no match for them; they were sophisticated, dressed in their finery. I was wearing my one and only civilian outfit, using scrounged clothing coupons from the family, a linen-like green and white patterned two-piece suit and flat brown and white moccasin-style shoes. My overcoat was at least 6 years old, its lining frayed and worn and its cuffs bare of material.

Once, as I was being seated opposite Scotty at a table in a London restaurant, the waiter took my coat off my shoulders with a flourish and I blushed as my torn and threadbare lining was displayed for all the world to see. A friend of mine had a similar experience when the waiter had taken her coat and lovingly draped it across the back of her chair, displaying the improvised padding she had used to give it up-to-date, military-style shoulders. There for all the patrons to see where two white sanitary pads, loops and all.

Being taken to restaurants and hotels with Scotty made me realize just how little I knew about fine food. War broke out in 1939 when I was 14. rationing began and prior to that time we had not, as a family, ever frequented restaurants known for their cuisine; our food had been wholesome but very ordinary fare. For the past three years RAF food had also been nourishing, wholesome and plentiful but we were certainly not given *cordon bleu* food. When I was offered the menu, Scotty watched me as I tried to make up my mind what to have. I was embarrassed, some terms I did not know and other dishes I did not know how to tackle. For instance, lobster or crab was often on the menu. How did one get at the meat? How did one hold the claws and attack them without making a mess? So I would say "I'll have the lemon sole," and then looking longingly at the succulent crab or lobster other patrons were enjoying.

I didn't want to reveal my ignorance, especially as I felt from remarks such as "Do you ride Smith?" or "Have you an evening dress?" that Scotty and I were very much from 'different sides of the track'. On dates back at camp we usually went "Dutch" and more often than not settled for a hearty fish-and-chip or sausage-and-egg dinner, which at the time we thought delicious.

After a 48-hour pass home I joined the Sunday night scramble at Paddington Railway Station. It was noisy and boisterous. Many of us would used the same ticket for weeks, pushing past the flustered ticket collector, holding up our faded tickets or en masse as he tried to grapple with the outstretched hands tightly clutching the worn and torn paper.

There was one unfortunate incident when the triumphant ticket collector "caught one", his culprit standing by his side looking very embarrassed. As we neared the gate we were shocked and amazed to find his captive was none other than our station Adjutant! But we all thought, "There for the Grace of God go I…"

Back at the office at Medmenham I was often called to be 'escort' for a prisoner.

"Smith, you're wanted for Escort duty," the corporal would shout and I would hastily brush my hair, put on my hat, rub my shoes on the back of my stockinged leg and present myself at the door.

"Fall in, left-right-left-right, right wheel, mark time," and the stiff-backed NCO would march into the Officer's room and give details of the defaulter's crime.

On the order "Prisoner and escort forward march" we would step into the office to face the officer.

We looked straight ahead as the officer read out the crime and subsequent sentence and then we would be 'about-faced' and 'dismissed' and out into the fresh air and sunshine again. I never liked being an escort, but I was the obvious choice, being near and available. As for my own charge sheet, I have never seen it, but I think it was nearly snow-white. Anything I was caught for was not breaking any hard-and-fast rules and often just a small jankers duty would be given. For instance, I was caught for having my hair touching my collar. I started off my WAAF career with long wavy hair and tucked it up into a skein of wool to keep it tidy and off my collar, but later I wore it short. I cut it short myself. There was in fact a very good hairdresser on camp and she made the girls hair really nice with waves and styles, but I preferred to look after my own hair.

I had been to see Ingrid Bergman in the film *For Whom The Bell Tolls*. Ingrid had her hair short about her head and I loved the look. One night while getting ready for a date, I got out the scissors and, standing before the mirror in our hut, chopped my longish hair short all over my head. It curled wildly and I was pleased with the result, it was easy to care for, my hat sat on my head better, although I don't think my date for the night was at all pleased – he didn't recognize me!

As at Chicksands Priory, with the war ended in Europe there was not the same urgency to complete tasks, which were humdrum and just day-to-day office routine and so, when eventually Group 59 came up for demobilization I was ready – or thought I was – to return to civilian life.

I was approached by one of the WAAF officers, who asked me if I would be prepared to sign on and to go to OCTU (Officers Training). I was flattered but it was August 1947, nearly 8 years since the war had started. I had been in school uniform for 3 years, sparse clothes (with rationing) during my first working jobs and then nearly four years in the uniform of the WAAF.

"Sorry Ma'am," I replied, "I really would like to get into civvy street and buy some pretty clothes." I think she thought I was being very flighty

I had been stationed at Medmenham 90 Group RAF station for over a year. The work had been reasonably interesting and I liked working with the CO and Adj. Danny, one of the Jamaican airmen in the office was a pleasure to work with. He was always very willing to do any of the jobs he was given and I loved his West Indian accent. He would come into the office and say, "Give me that Finchley smile, Smithy," and that, said in his accent would always make me smile. I don't know if he returned to Jamaica or married and remained in England. I do know that many of the Jamaicans at East Kirkby felt the cold terribly; especially when it snowed and the icy winds blew across the flat straight fenland of Lincolnshire.

I had mixed feelings. I had enjoyed particularly the comradeship and the freedom of being in the WAAF. I joined a quiet, thin girl, but three and a half years later I was more mature, more sure of myself, knew who I was and was full of confidence. In my small way I felt I had contributed something to the war effort. It was an opportunity I had seized with both hands and I wouldn't have missed it for all the world.

Once more, and for the last time, I went round the station with my clearance chit, had my Pay Book stamped and was issued later at Dispersal Centre Kirkham with a travel warrant, coupons etc … and from that moment on I was no longer 'WAAF 298 Smith' or 'Smithy'.

I put away my WAAF cap, combed my hair out of its tight roll and into shoulder-length style, slipped on my earrings, pulled on my one and only pair of silk stockings and stepped into my high-heeled shoes.

Miss Eileen Smith had returned.

The Author with Elsie, a friend from Hut 6602, RAF Medmenham.

The grounds at RAF Medmenham.

8. PostScript

Back in Civvy Street there seemed to be an emptiness to my life. I missed the companionship of the people I had worked with, the friendships and shared confidences, the boys who were special to me, the jokes and the feeling of belonging. You were never alone unless you wished to be, always had someone to go to the pictures with, or out for a meal or just for a walk. Suddenly, I had to pick up the threads of the life I had lived before I joined, something I had in common with millions of other ex-servicemen and women.

Friends I had known before I joined had married, moved away or grown away from me; we had nothing in common anymore. There was no one to share my experiences or to understand them.

My old job was still there for me but, four years later I was much more experienced in all manner of things and was capable of being more than just a junior secretary at the same rate of pay I had been getting before, so I said 'no thank you'.

Being in Group 59 for demobilization, by the time I got out of the WAAF most of the good job vacancies had been filled. Eventually, I did get a job and it was a pleasure to have a good pay packet, which I could spend on new clothes, make up etc, clothing coupons being the only restriction on buying. I cruised the shops in Tottenham Court Road in South Kensington, buying blouses, skirts, a coat, nice underwear and shoes from Dolcies.

I found that the independence I gained in the WAAF stood me in good stead; I was no longer the quiet, shy girl I had been before the WAAF.

I have kept in touch for the last 50 years with Elsie, my Post Office Corporal at Chicksands and within minutes of meeting, no matter how much time has elapsed between visits, we are back into our easy ways of laughing, ribbing and joking.

I now live in Australia, am married and have two children and seven grandchildren. My husband and I (I sound like the Queen) have joined the British Ex-Services Association and once a month we have a get together. We feel the old camaraderie of our service days, understand each other's jokes and talk about our experiences.

We march on Australia's special day ANZAC Australian and New Zealand Services, representing various sections of the British Services and honouring the men and women who joined and who did not come back. We also remember our friends of those days and wonder how they are.

A few years ago I wrote an article in a UK magazine recalling my days spent in Lincolnshire and wondered in the article what had become of East Kirkby RAF Station. Had the fields gone back to the farmers and were sheep and cows now grazing on them? I received many letters telling me that an Aviation Centre was now at EK and about the wonderful job that brothers Fred and Harold Panton, in memory of their broth Chris who was lost in a bombing raid, had done. The brothers have restored the

Control Tower, which over the years had gone into decay and they also have a Lancaster, which can be taken out of the Hangar and the engines revved up. There are pictures of WAAF and RAF on boards in the hanger from all over the country.

Whilst staying with friends Les and Grace Walker, who live in Sandy near EK, my husband and I visited the Aviation Centre and it was real thrill to be there again, driving along those familiar roads, past the Red Lion and past where the WAAF compound had been. We had a cup of tea at the NAAFI and looked at all the articles there for sale or to look at.

We went to the restored Control Tower and were amazed at the work which had gone into making the Tower come alive again with the voiceovers, signs on the walls and lifelike figures. We joined other visitors out on the tarmac where the Lancaster had been wheeled out. We fell silent as the engines gradually started to rev up and then roared; we just stood and listened, remembering the EK of all those years ago.

We left the old airfield and took the road to Boston where I revisited the square where we used to pile out of our buses, airmen and airwomen from all parts of the world dressed in all shades of blue before making for the dances, the cafés and the pubs. I took a few more photos and put them, on my return to Australia, along with other photos I had managed to keep from my WAAF days.

Smithy

End

"Why did we join? Why did we join?
Why did we join the Royal Air Force?
Ten bob a week. Nothing to eat.
Damn great boots making blisters on your feet…"

These were the words to a song that Eileen Smith and her pals in the WAAF (Women's Auxiliary Air Force) used to sing under their breath as they route-marched round the country lanes near Wilmslow whilst on basic training.

Eileen answers the question herself in this charming and nostalgic book. She, and thousands like her, joined the WAAF during World War II in order to 'do their bit' for the war effort. The facilities were Spartan, the work less than glamorous, but they all knew that it was worthwhile. They also enjoyed a strong bond of camaraderie that none of them would ever forget.

After basic training – interrupted by a spell in hospital with suspected TB – Eileen (known as 'Smithy' to her service pals) was posted to RAF East Kirkby, an operational Bomber Command Station, home to 57 and 630 Squadrons and their Lancaster heavy bombers, in which the aircrews would take off almost nightly to mount raids on Nazi-occupied Europe, many of them never to return.

The excitement, the danger and the close proximity of numerous young men and women led to a uniquely emotionally-charged atmosphere and inevitably, many romantic liaisons flourished. Some would end tragically, others would be fleeting and light-hearted, others still would endure for a lifetime.

Eileen recaptures her far-off WAAF days with a clarity and a sense of humour that make this book both highly entertaining and a historically valuable account of a unique period in history.

ISBN 1-903953-53-7

9 781903 953532 >

UK Price £9.95

www.woodfieldpublishing.com